iPhone 12 User

Complete and Illustrated Manual with Tips and Tricks to Master Your iPhone 12. For Beginners and New Users

Nobert Young

Copyright @ 2020

Table of Content

Introduction

Apple announced iPhone 12 on Tuesday, October 13, 2020 – the world's most powerful smartphone currently. The phone comes loaded with iOS 14, Apple's latest operating system.

iOS 14 is one of the biggest iOS updates that Apple has made to date. The update brought about several new features and tweaks like the translation app, the sleep tracking app, Siri improvements, and several others.

With the Picture-in-Picture feature, you can watch videos or make FaceTime calls on your iPhone while surfing the net or reading your Messages.

On the Messages app, you can pin conversations from your favorite people to the top of the Message screen. There is also the @mention feature, which sends a notification to a group participant when the user's name is mentioned.

App Clips allow you to use an app's features without downloading and installing the app – you can make a restaurant reservation, pay for a parking ticket, order for pizza, etc., just by scanning the merchant code on your phone.

There is the App Library that organizes your apps into different categories like Entertainment, Social, and so on. You can choose to have all your apps in the App Library alone or keep the apps in both the App Library and the Home Screen.

Users can now add different widgets to the home screen. A new widget called the SmartStack combines different widgets and then shows you a widget per time, based on the time, activity, and location.

With the Digital car keys feature, you can unlock and start your car using your Apple Watch or iPhone.

Use the Translate app to translate voice and text in 11 different languages online and offline.

The iPhone has never been as powerful as it is now. This user guide includes all the tips and tricks you need to operate your iPhone 12 on iOS 14.

Chapter 1: Getting Started

Set up iPhone

- Press and hold the side button until the Apple Logo appears.

- Choose your **Language** and **Country/ Region.**

- Tap **Set up Manually,** then proceed with the prompt on your screen.

- But if you have another iPhone, iPod Touch, or iPad, you can use **Quick Start** to set up your new iPhone automatically. Place the two devices beside each other, then proceed with the instructions on your screen to securely copy the settings, iCloud Keychain, and preferences from the old device to the new iPhone. You can then choose to restore the remaining data to your new device from your iCloud back up.

- You can also choose to wirelessly transfer all your data from your other device to the new iPhone. Ensure that the devices are close to each other and plugged into power until the transfer is complete.

Hello

Quick Start

Bring your current iPhone or iPad near this
iPhone to sign in and set up.

If your other iPhone or iPad doesn't show
options for setting up this iPhone, make
sure it's running iOS 11 or later, and has
Bluetooth turned on. You can also set up
this iPhone manually.

Set Up Manually

- If you have low vision or blind, triple-tap the side button to turn on
  VoiceOver. VoiceOver will then walk you through the steps.

Move Data from Android to iPhone

Besides transferring content from other iOS or iPadOS devices, you can also
move from an Android device. Note that you can only use this option when
setting up your iPhone for the first time or after you erase your phone.

Before you begin,

- Turn on Wi-Fi on both devices.

- Plug both devices into power.

- Confirm that you have sufficient space on the new iPhone.

- Go to Google Play Store on your Android and download the **Move to iOS** app.

Then follow the steps below to transfer content between the two devices:

- Power on the new iPhone and follow the setup assistant until you get to the **Apps & Data** screen, then click **Move Data from Android.**

- Open the Move to iOS app on your Android device and tap **Continue.** Go through the terms and conditions, then tap **Agree.** Tap **Next** in the upper right corner of the **Find Your Code** screen.

- Tap **Continue** on your iPhone, then wait for the code to show. Enter the code on your Android device.

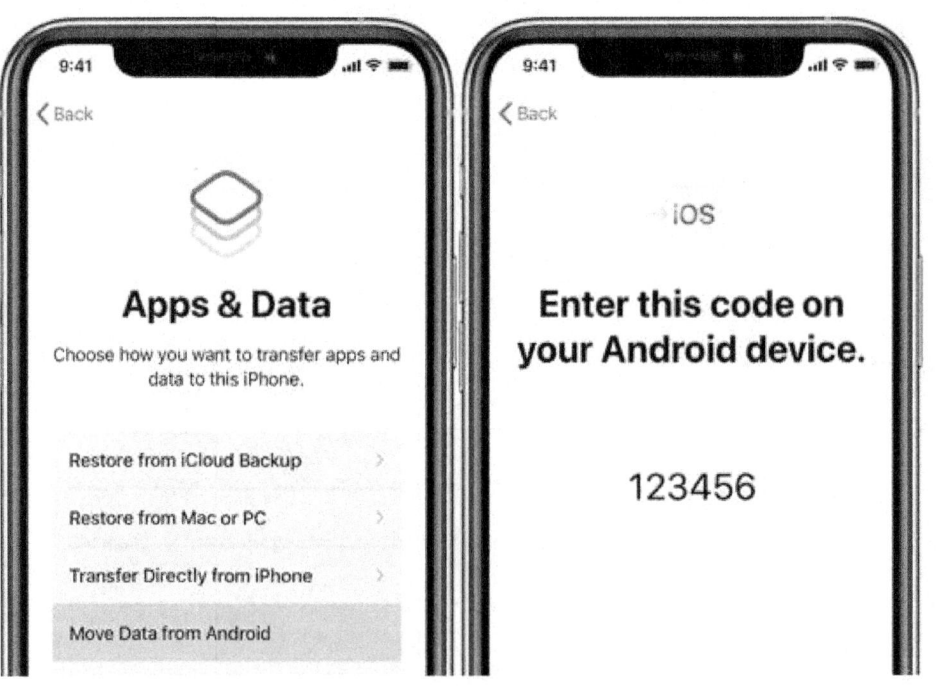

- Select the content that you wish to move and then tap **Next.** Wait for the loading bar on your iOS screen to finish, then tap **Done** on the Android and **Continue** on the iPhone.

- Proceed with the prompts on your iPhone screen to finish setting up your iOS device.

Set up Cellular Service with eSIM

To use the cellular connection on your iOS device, you need to have a SIM card. You can also use an eSIM on your device. The eSIM is stored digitally on your phone. To set up,

- Go to Settings, tap **Cellular,** and then click **Add Cellular Plan.**

- Use your phone camera to capture the QR code provided by your carrier or enter the details manually. You may need to enter a confirmation code provided by your service provider.

- Then click **Add Cellular Plan.** If the eSIM is your second line, proceed with the instructions on your screen to set up the SIM.

You can have more than one eSIMs on your iPhone, but you can only use one eSIM per time. To switch eSIMs,

- Go to Settings, tap **Cellular,** select the plan you want, then click **Turn on This Line.**

Manage Cellular Plans

If you have two SIMs on your iPhone, you can choose how you want your phone to use each SIM.

- Go to Settings, tap **Cellular,** click **Cellular Data,** and choose a default line for your cellular data. Turn on **Allow Cellular Data Switching** to permit the phone to use any of the lines depending on availability and coverage.

- To choose a default line for voice calls, tap **Default Voice Line.**
- Scroll to **Cellular Plans,** select a line and then change settings like Wi-Fi calling, Cellular Plan Label, SIM Pin, or Calls on Other Devices.

Note that if using dual SIM, you must turn on Wi-Fi calling for a line if you want that line to receive calls while the other line is on a call.

Sign in with Your Apple ID

Your Apple ID is an account you use to access all Apple services like Apple Books, FaceTime, iMessage, iCloud, and so on. When setting up your phone, you will receive the prompt to sign in to Apple ID. If you skipped the step at setup, you could follow the steps below to sign in at any time.

- Go to Settings and tap **Sign in to your iPhone.**
- Input your Apple ID and password or create a new one.
- If you secured your account with 2-factor authentication, you would need to enter the verification code to finish.

Change Apple ID Settings

- Go to Settings and tap your name.
- You can then change your password, update your contact information, or manage family sharing.

Change your iCloud Settings

Use iCloud to securely store your documents, videos, apps, music, and more. It also helps to keep all your connected devices up to date.

- Go to Settings, tap your name, and click **iCloud.**

26

- On the next screen, you will see your iCloud storage status. You have free 5G storage. To upgrade the storage, click **Manage Storage,** then select **Change Storage Plan.**

- On this same screen, you can turn on features that should work with iCloud like Photos, Messages, Contacts, etc.

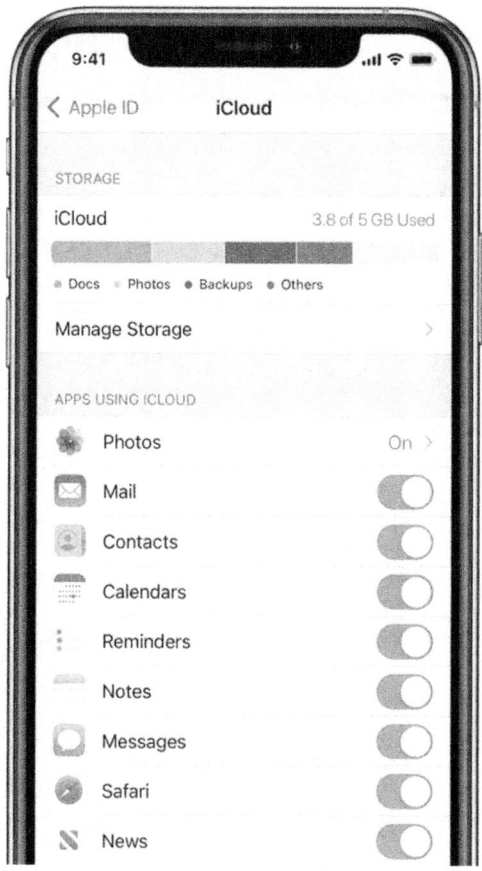

Connect to a Wi-Fi Network

- Go to Settings, tap **Wi-Fi,** and then turn on Wi-Fi.

- Select a Wi-Fi network, input the password if required, or tap **Others** to join a hidden network.

- The icon at the top of your screen confirms that your phone is connected to a Wi-Fi network.

Wake iPhone

Use any of the steps below to wake your iPhone,

- Tap the screen and press the side button.
- Raise your iPhone. To turn off this option, go to **Settings,** tap **Display & Brightness,** then disable **Raise to Wake.**

Unlock iPhone

See the chapter on how to create a passcode. To unlock with a passcode,

- Swipe up from the end of the lock screen.
- Then input the passcode.

To unlock with Face ID

- Raise your iPhone or tap the screen, then stare into your phone to unlock it.
- Swipe up from the bottom of your screen to go to the home screen.
- Press the side button to lock the iPhone. Note that the phone locks automatically if left idle for a minute or more.

Set Sound and Vibration Options

You can choose the sound your phone plays when you have a call, email, reminder, etc. You can also customize your vibration options.

- Go to Settings, and tap **Sounds & Haptics.**
- Drag the slider under **Ringers and Alerts** to change the volume for all sounds.

- To set the vibration and tones patterns for sounds, click a sound type like text tone or ringtone, then scroll through the tones and click one to use it. Click **Vibration** and select a vibration pattern or tap **Create New Vibration** to make yours.

Customize Haptic Feedback

Haptic feedback is the tap or quick vibration you feel when you perform actions like change settings, using the flashlights, etc.

- Go to Settings, tap **Sounds & Haptics,** then disable or enable **System Haptics.**
- If you disable System Haptics, you won't feel or hear vibrations for incoming alerts and notifications.

Customize Dark Mode

Dark Mode makes your phone display change to a dark color scheme suitable for low-light environments. You can manually turn on Dark Mode or set it to come on automatically at defined times. Best for using your phone when reading in bed. There are two ways to turn this on

- Open the Control center and press firmly on , then tap to enable or disable dark mode.
- Go to **Settings,** tap **Display & Brightness,** choose **Dark** to enable Dark Mode, or **Light** to disable it.
- If you want it to come on automatically, toggle on **Automatic,** then click **Options.**
- Choose **Custom Schedule** or **Sunset to Sunrise.** Use Custom Schedule to set the times you want Dark Mode to work or not work.

Screen Brightness

You can adjust your bright brightness manually or automatically.

To adjust manually,

- Open the control center and pull to the left or right. Or,

- Go to Settings, tap **Display & Brightness,** then pull the slider left or right.

iPhone can also adjust the screen brightness automatically using the current light conditions:

- Go to Settings, tap **Accessibility,** click **Display & Text Size,** and turn on **Auto-Brightness.**

True Tone

True Tune automatically adapts the intensity and color of your screen display to match the light in your environment. You can turn it on or off in two ways:

- Open the Control center and press firmly on , then tap to enable or disable True Tone.

- Go to **Settings,** tap **Display & Brightness,** then enable or disable **True Tone.**

Night Shift

Night Shift adjusts the colors in your display, making it warmer and friendly to the eyes when using your phone at night or in dark places. You can turn it on manually or automatically. To turn on manually,

- Open the Control center and press firmly on , then tap to enable.

To schedule night shift and have it come on automatically,

- Go to **Settings,** tap **Display & Brightness,** and then tap **Night Shift.**

- Toggle on **Scheduled,** then drag the slider under **Color Temperature** left or right to adjust the color balance for Night Shift.

- Click **From** and choose either **Custom Schedule** or **Sunset to Sunrise.**

Change your iPhone Name

Changing your device name makes it easy to find when sharing hotspots and the lines.

- Go to Settings, tap **General,** tap **About,** and then tap **Name.**

- Tap , enter a new name, and then click **Done.**

Set Time and Date

- Go to Settings, tap **General,** and tap **Date & Time.**

- Select **Set Automatically** to allow the iPhone to choose the time and date using your current location.

- Turn on **24 Hour Time** if you want the iPhone to display the hours from 0 to 23.

- To manually change the time and date, toggle off **Set Automatically,** then enter the time and date.

Chapter 2: Basic Settings

Restart iPhone

Restart your phone if it isn't responding to taps and clicks:

First is to turn off the phone

- Press firmly on any of the volume buttons and the side buttons until you see the power off slider, then drag the slider to power off the phone.

- Alternatively, go to **Settings,** tap **General,** tap **Shut Down,** and then pull the **Power Off** slider.

Next is to turn the iPhone back on. To do this,

- Press and hold the side button until you see the Apple logo.

Force Restart an iPhone

- Quickly press and release the volume up button. Do the same for the volume down button.

- Then press and hold the side button until the Apple logo appears before you release the button.

Update iPhone Automatically

See how to turn on automatic updates

- Go to **Settings,** tap **General,** and then tap **Software Update.**

- Click on **Customize Automatic Updates** or **Automatic Updates.** Then choose to download and install new updates automatically. Come back here to disable automatic updates.

- With this setting, whenever there is a new update, your phone downloads and installs the update at night when charging your phone.

Manually Update Phone

To check for new updates manually,

- Go to **Settings,** tap **General,** and then tap **Software Update.**
- You will see the currently installed iOS version and any update.

Update Using Your Computer

You can also connect your phone to your computer and use the computer to update your phone:

- Use a USB device to connect your computer and iPhone.
- If using a Mac, go to the Finder sidebar and click on your iPhone, tap **General** at the top of the window, then click on **Check for Update.**
- If using a Windows PC, open the iTunes app, tap the iPhone button close to the top left side of the iTunes window, tap **Summary,** and then click on **Check for Update.**
- Follow the instructions on your screen to finish.
- Click **Update** to install an update.

Back up iPhone using your Mac

- Use a USB device to connect your computer and iPhone.
- Go to the Finder sidebar and click on your iPhone, tap **General** at the top of the window, then click on **Back up all of the data on your iPhone to this Mac.**

- Click on **Encrypt Local Backup** if you wish to protect your backup with a password.

- Tap **Backup Now** to finish.

To back up using your Windows PC,

- Open the iTunes app on your computer, tap the iPhone button close to the top left side of the iTunes window, tap **Summary,** and then click on **Back up Now.**

- Click on **Encrypt Local Backup** if you wish to protect your backup with a password. Enter the password and tap **Set Password.**

Backup iPhone using iCloud

You can backup your phone using iCloud service:

- Go to Settings, tap your name, tap **iCloud,** and then click on **iCloud Backup.**

- Enable **iCloud Backup** and iCloud will automatically back up your phone when it's on Wi-Fi and locked or connected to power.

- Tap **Back up Now** to perform a manual backup.

To view your iCloud backups,

- Go to Settings, tap your name, tap **iCloud,** click on **Manage Storage,** then select **Backups.**

- To delete a backup, tap the backup from the list and then tap **Delete Backup.**

Return iPhone to its Default Settings

You can return your phone to the default without erasing the content on the phone. Ensure to back up your phone before you perform a reset.

- Go to **Settings,** tap **General,** and then click on **Reset.**

- Click on **Reset All Settings** to reset all settings – including home screen layout, privacy settings, keyboard dictionary, and Apple Pay cards – to their default.

- Tap **Reset Home Screen Layout** to return the built-in apps to their default layout on the Home Screen.

- Tap **Reset Keyboard Dictionary** to erase all the words you added.

- Tap **Reset Network Settings** to remove all the network settings.

- Tap **Reset Location & Privacy** to reset the privacy settings and location services to their defaults.

Erase an iPhone

Erase your phone to remove all its settings and content stored on the phone, mostly when you want to give the phone away.

- Go to Settings, click on **General,** and then tap **Reset.**

- Enter your passcode or Apple ID password if requested, then click on **Erase All Content and Settings.**

- When the phone restarts, you will see the option to restore a backup or to set up your phone as new.

Use a Computer to Erase your iPhone

You can use a Windows PC or Mac to erase your iPhone, install the latest iOS version, and restore iPhone to factory settings. Before the computer erases your phone, you will see the option to create a backup.

- Use a USB device to connect your computer and iPhone.

- If using a Mac, go to the Finder sidebar and click on your iPhone, tap **General**, then click on **Restore iPhone.**

- If using a Windows PC, open the iTunes app, tap the iPhone button close to the top left side of the iTunes window, tap **Summary,** then click on **Restore iPhone.**

- Proceed with the instructions on your screen to finish.

Restore iPhone from an iCloud Backup

- Turn on the new iPhone and proceed with the instructions on your screen to choose a region and language.

- Tap **Set up Manually,** click on **Restore from iCloud Backup,** and then proceed with the instructions on your screen.

Restore iPhone from a Computer Backup

- Use a USB device to connect your computer and iPhone.

- If using a Mac, go to the Finder sidebar, click on your iPhone, and tap **Trust.**

- If using a Windows PC, open the iTunes app, tap the device icon close to the top left side of your screen, and choose your iPhone from the list.

- Tap **Restore from This Backup,** select the backup and then tap **Continue.**

Chapter 3: Family Sharing

Family sharing allows family members to share subscriptions, purchases, screen time information, iCloud storage plan, and more without sharing their accounts. One adult, called the organizer, creates the group, adds up to five other family members, and then chooses the features that the family can share. Once the other family members accept the invitation to join the group, Family Sharing is automatically set up on their devices.

Set Up Family Sharing

- Go to Settings on your phone and tap your name.
- Click on **Family Sharing,** then follow the instructions on your screen to set up your group. You get to add the different family members or even create an account for your child.
- Select the features you wish to share, then continue with the instructions on your screen.

Add a Family Member

Only the organizer of the group can add family members

- Go to Settings on your phone and tap your name.
- Click on **Family Sharing,** tap **Add Member,** and then tap **Invite People.**
- Continue with the instructions on your screen to complete.

Create Apple ID for a Child

Only two people can create Apple ID for a child. The organizer of the group or the person created as the Parent or Guardian by the organizer.

To create Apple ID for your child,

- Go to Settings, tap your name, and click on **Family Sharing.**
- As the guardian or parent, click on **Add Child,** then proceed with the instructions on your screen.
- As the group organizer, click on **Add Member,** tap **Create an Account for a Child,** then proceed with the instructions on your screen.

View and Adjust Group Sharing Settings

You can change the sharing settings at any time.

- Go to Settings, tap your name, and click on **Family Sharing.**
- To set up a new feature, tap the feature, and proceed with the instructions on your screen.
- To review an existing feature, tap the feature and adjust the sharing settings as you like.

Disable Family Sharing

You can choose to leave or even disband the family sharing group at any time.

- Go to Settings, tap your name, and click on **Family Sharing.**
- Tap your name again, then tap **Stop Using Family Sharing** to leave the group or tap **Stop Using Family** to disband the group.

Note that it is only the organizer that can disband a group.

Remove Someone from the Family Group

The group organizer can only remove persons from age 13 and above. But you can transfer a child to another family. To remove someone,

- Go to Settings, tap your name, and click on **Family Sharing.**
- Click on the family member you wish to remove, then select **Remove (Family Member) From Family.**

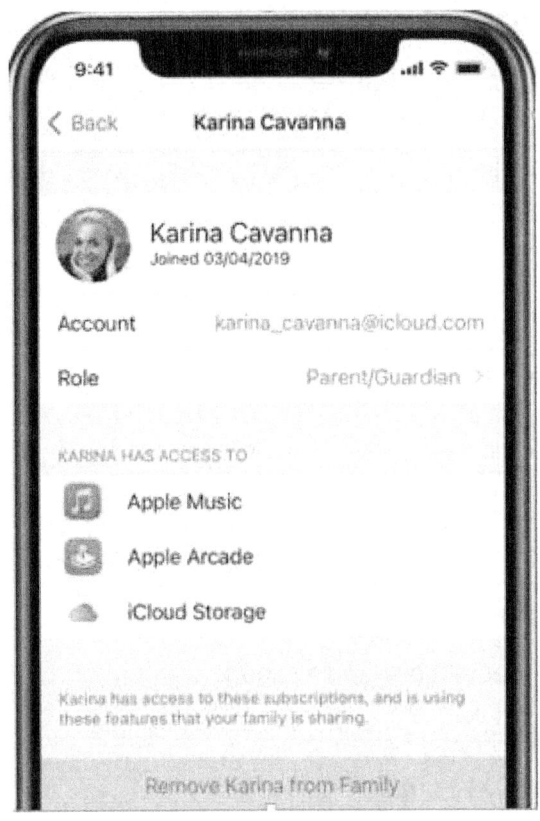

Move a Child to another Family Sharing Group

The only way to remove a child under 13 years from a family sharing group is to move the child to another group. To do this, ask the second family group's organizer to invite the child to their family. Once they send the request, you will get an invitation. Follow the steps below to approve the request:

- Go to Settings, tap your name, and click on **Invitations.**
- Then approve the invitation.

Invite a Child to Your Family

- Go to Settings, tap your name, and click on **Family Sharing.**

- Tap **Add Family Member,** tap **Invite in Person** and then proceed with the instructions on your screen.

- Ask the organizer to approve the child's transfer to your group.

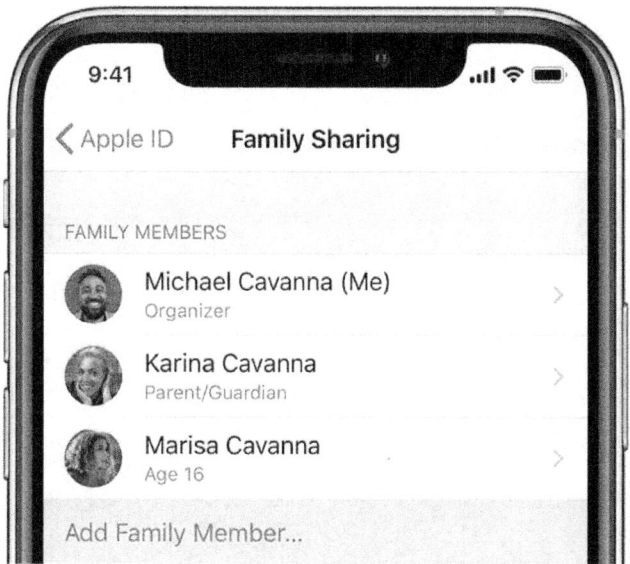

Download Family Members' Purchases

Every purchase by members of a family group is charged to the organizer's Apple ID account. The organizer can also request that children in the group get approval before making purchases or free download. When a family member purchases an item, the item is added to their account, while eligible purchases are made available for other family members to download.

To download shared purchases from the iTunes store,

- Open iTunes Store, click on **More** and then tap **Purchased.**

- Select the family member and click on a category.

- Select the purchased item and tap ☁️ to download.

To download shared purchases from the app store,

- Open the App Store and tap your profile picture or the ⊙ icon at the top right.

- Tap **Purchased,** select the family member, and then tap ☁ beside the purchased item to download.

To download from Apple Books

- Open the Apple Books app and tap your profile picture or the ⊙ icon at the top right.

- Navigate to **Family Purchases** and click on the family member, then choose a category.

- Tap **Recent Purchases, Genre,** or **All,** then tap ☁ beside the purchased item to download.

To download from the Apple TV app,

- Launch the Apple TV app, tap **Library,** click on **Family Sharing,** and select a family member.

- Click on a genre or category, tap the purchased content, and then tap ☁ to download.

Stop Sharing Purchases with Family Members

Teen and adult family members may decide not to share purchases and with other members of the family by turning off purchase sharing for themselves.

- Go to Settings, tap your name, and click on **Family Sharing.**

- Click on **Purchase Sharing** and then disable **Share Purchases with Family.**

- The organizer can click on **Stop Purchase Sharing** to stop sharing purchases completely.

Enable Ask to Buy for Children

This option means that the organizer, parent, or guardian needs to approve all the purchases done by the children in a Family Sharing group:

- Go to Settings, tap your name, and click on **Family Sharing.**
- Click on **Ask to Buy,** tap the child's name, and then toggle on **Ask to Buy.**
- If there is no child in the group, click on **Create a Child Account** or **Add Child,** then proceed with the instructions on your screen.

Set Up Apple Cash Family

The family sharing group organizer can create an Apple Cash account for a child in the group and then use the Wallet app to monitor transactions, view card balance, and limit the persons that the child can send money to.

- Go to Settings, tap your name, and click on **Family Sharing.**
- Click on **Apple Cash,** tap the child's name, click on Set up Apple Cash, and then proceed with the instructions on your screen.

Share iCloud Storage and Subscriptions with Family Members

You can share subscriptions to different channels with other members of the family.

- Go to Settings, tap your name, and click on **Family Sharing.**
- Click on a subscription and proceed with the prompts on your screen.

Share Your Location with Family Members

If the organizer sets up location sharing when creating the Family Sharing group, the organizer's location will be shared automatically. Other members of the family can also choose to share their location if desired. Sharing your location will help other family members locate your missing device, as well as see your location in the Find My app. Before you can share your location, you need to turn on **Location Services** in the Settings app of your phone. To enable location services,

- Go to Settings, click on Privacy, and then turn on **Location Services.**

Now continue with the steps below to turn on share your location with your family members:

- Go to Settings, tap your name, and click on **Family Sharing.**
- Tap **Location Sharing,** and then enable **Share My Location.**
- If you are yet to share your location, click on **Use this iPhone as my Location.**
- Choose the family member you want to share your location with, and then click on **Share My Location.** Do this for all the family members that should see your location.
- To stop sharing your location with a member, click on the family member, and then select **Stop Sharing my Location.**

Here is another way to share or send your location with family members:

- Open the Messages app and open a conversation with a family member.

- Tap the name or profile picture of the family member at the top of your screen.

- Tap and then choose **Share My Location** or **Send My Current Location.**

Set up Your iPhone to be found by a Family Member

For your family member to help find your missing device, you need to do the following:

- Turn on **Find My iPhone:** go to Settings, tap your name, click **Find My,** select **Find My iPhone,** then toggle on **Find My Network, Find My iPhone** and **Send Last Location.**

- Turn on Location Services: Go to Settings, click on **Privacy**, and then turn on **Location Services.**

- Share your location with family members: Go to Settings, tap your name, click on **Family Sharing**, tap **Location Sharing,** and then toggle on **Share My Location.**

If all these settings are on, follow the steps below to locate a missing device:

- Tap **Devices** in the Find My app, then click on the missing device. Your family member's device will come under yours.

- The device location will appear on the map. But if the device cannot be located, you will see the **No Location Found** message under the name of the device.

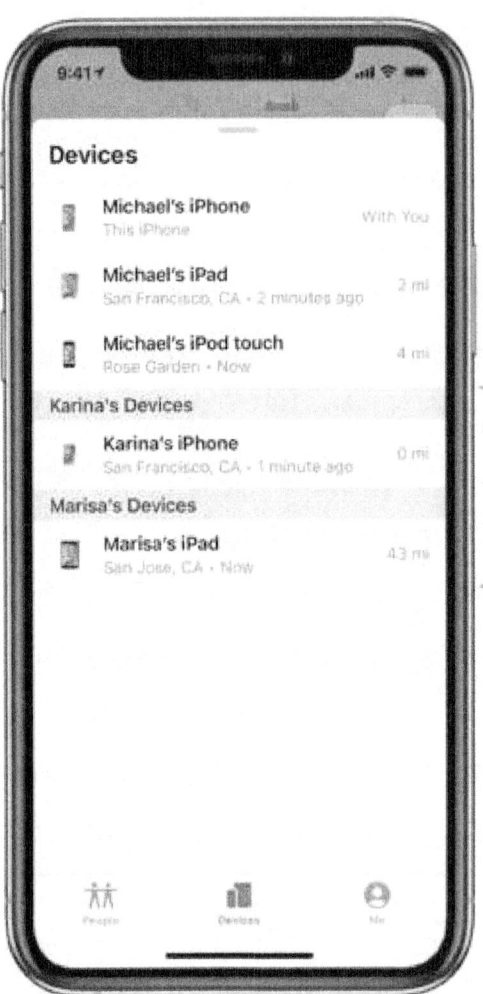

Family members' devices appear below yours.

Chapter 4: Screen Time

Use Screen Time to set limits and allowances for app use, schedule app downtimes, and more.

Turn on Screen Time and Set Downtime

Downtime ensures that you do not receive notifications or access apps on your phone during a selected period.

- Go to Settings, tap **Screen Time,** and then click on **Turn on Screen Time.**
- Tap **Continue,** then click on **This is my iPhone.**
- Click on **Downtime,** and then toggle on **Downtime.**
- Choose either **Customize Days** or **Every Day,** then create the start and end times.

Set App Limits

This setting determines the amount of time that you can use the apps on your device. Follow this step after you have turned on Screen Time.

- Go to Settings, tap **Screen Time,** and then click on **App Limits.**
- Tap **Add Limit,** then choose one or more app categories. If you prefer to set the limit for individual apps, click on the category name to view the apps in that category, then choose the apps you want for that category.
- Tap **Next,** and set the allowed time for the selected apps. To choose time for different days, click on **Customize Days** and set limits for the different days.

- To limit more apps or categories, tap **Choose Apps,** and repeat the steps above.
- Once done, tap **Add** to go back to the Apps Limit screen.

Temporarily Turn Off App Limits

To disable the app limits for a defined period,

- Go to Settings on your phone, tap **Screen Time,** and then click on **App Limits.**
- Click on a category and select **App Limit** to turn off a limit temporarily.
- If you wish to remove the limit for that category permanently, tap **Delete Limit.**

Set Communication Limits

Communication Limits involves blocking outgoing and incoming communications like phone calls and messages from specific contacts in iCloud at selected periods or at all times.

The first step is to enable **Contacts** in iCloud. To do this,

- Go to Settings, tap your name, tap **iCloud,** and then enable **Contacts.**

Once done, proceed with the steps below to set communication limits:

- Go to Settings, tap **Screen Time,** then click on **Communication Limits.**
- If you want this limit at all times, click on **During Screen Time,** and then choose who the limit should apply to – **Everyone, Contacts & Groups with at Least One Contact,** or **Contacts Only.**
- To limit communication during downtime, click on **During Downtime.** You will notice that the option for **During Screen time** is selected automatically. However, you can change it to **Specific**

Contacts, then select either **Add New Contact** or **Choose from My Contacts.**

Note that you can't contact or receive communication from any persons blocked by your communication limit settings. You can change the settings if you need to reach out to someone blocked by your communication limit settings.

Choose Apps to Allow at All Times

You can set up the apps that can bypass downtime and communication limits

- Go to Settings, tap **Screen Time,** and then click on **Always Allowed.**

- Tap or this to remove or add apps from the **Allowed App** list.

Setup Screen Time and Downtime Your Family Member

To set up Screen Time and downtime limits for a family member,

- Go to Settings on the family member's device, tap **Screen Time,** and then click on **Turn on Screen Time.**

- Tap **Continue,** then click on **This is My Child's iPhone.**

- To create downtime for the child, choose the start and end times, and then click on **Set Downtime.**

- To create an apps limit for your family member, choose the categories (To see all the categories, click on **Show All Categories**). Tap **Set,** choose the amount of time for the limit, and then tap **Set App Limit.**

- Click on **Continue** and set up a Screen Time passcode for your child's Screen Time settings.

Set Communication Limits for a Child

The first step is to enable **Contacts** in iCloud. To do this,

- Go to Settings on the child's phone, tap the name, tap **iCloud,** and then enable **Contacts.**

Once done, proceed with the steps below to set communication limits:

- Go to Settings on their phone, tap **Screen Time,** and then click on **Communication Limits.**

- If you want this limit at all times, click on **During Screen Time,** and then choose who the limit should apply to – **Everyone, Contacts & Groups with at Least One Contact,** or **Contacts Only.**

- To limit communication during downtime, click on **During Downtime.** You will notice that the option for **During Screen time** is selected automatically. However, you can change to **Specific Contacts,** then select either **Add New Contact** or **Choose from My Contacts.**

- Click on **Allow Contact Editing** and enable or disable the option to allow or prevent your child from editing their contacts.

Set Content and Privacy Restrictions

Block inappropriate content from being displayed on your device (or your child's device) as well as set restrictions for App Store and iTunes store purchases. Note that the same settings apply to your child's device if you are managing it:

- Go to Settings on the phone (yours or the child), tap **Screen Time,** and then click on **Content & Privacy Restrictions.**

- Toggle on **Content & Privacy Restrictions** and then select options to create content allowances for App Store and iTunes Store purchases, content ratings, and so on.

- To stop someone in your family group from changing the maximum headphone volume, click on **Reduce Loud Sounds,** then choose **Don't Allow.**

Get Report of your Phone Use

See how to get a report of your device usage or that of a family member:

- Go to Settings on your phone, tap **Screen Time,** and then click on **See All Activity.**

- Click on **Day** to view a summary of your daily use and **Week** to see a weekly summary.

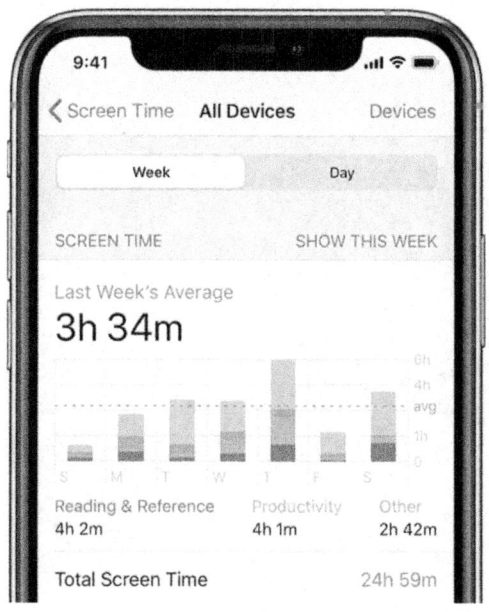

Chapter 5: Find My

You can use the Find My app to share your location, find a missing device, get direction to a family member, or wipe a lost device.

Set Up Location Sharing

Turn on Location Sharing on the Find My app to share your location with friends and family.

- Open the Find My app on your iPhone.

- Tap **Me** at the bottom, then toggle on **Share My Location.**

- You will find the device sharing your location in the **My Location** section. If your iPhone isn't sharing your location at the time, scroll down and click **Use this iPhone as My Location.**

Here is another way to change your location sharing settings:

- Open the Settings app and click on your name.

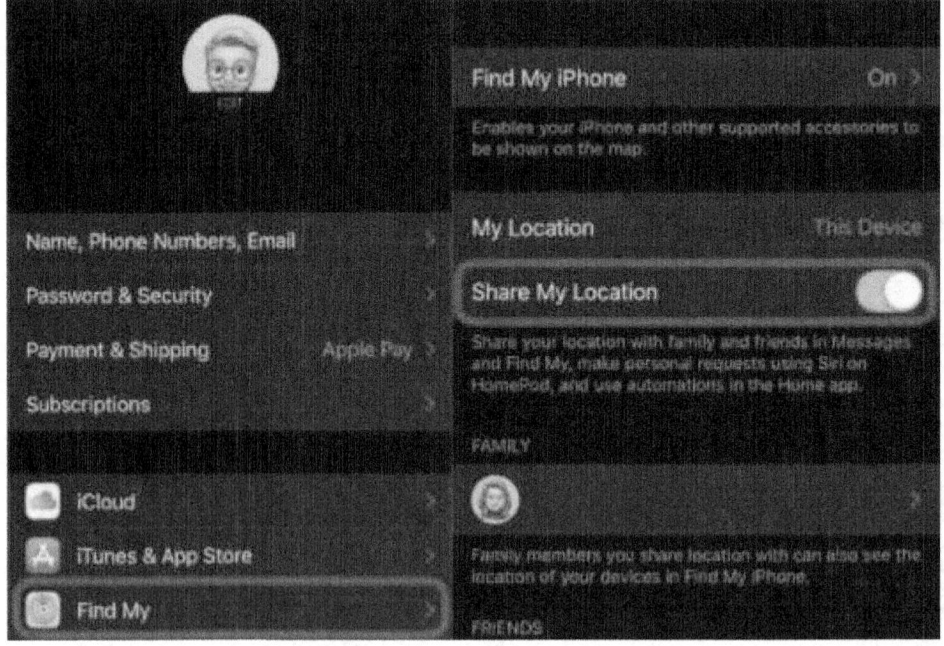

- Tap **Find My** and then toggle on **Share My Location**.

- Also, turn on **Find My iPhone** if it is disabled.

Set a Label for your Location

Create a label to show whether your current location is your home, work.

- Open the Find My app on your iPhone.

- Tap **Me,** then click on **Edit Location Name.**

- Choose the desired label. To add a different label from what is on the list, click on **Add Custom Label,** input a name, and then click on **Done.**

Share Your Location with a Friend

- Open the Find My app on your iPhone.

- Tap **People,** then scroll to the bottom of the list and click on **Share My Location**.

- Enter your friend's name in the **To** field or tap ⊕ and choose from your contact list.

- Click on **Send** & select the period you want the sharing to last for.

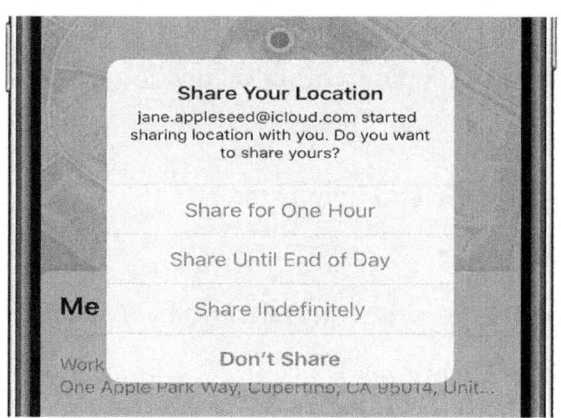

Stop Sharing your Location

See how to stop sharing your location with one person or hide your location from everyone.

- Open the Find My app on your iPhone.
- Tap **People,** then select the person you do not want to share your location with.
- Click on **Stop Sharing My Location,** then click on **Stop Sharing Location.**

To hide your location from everyone,

- Tap **Me,** then toggle off **Share My Location.**

Respond to a Location Sharing Request

A friend may send you a request to share your location with them.

- Open the Find My app and tap **People** at the bottom.
- Click on **Share** under the name of the person that sent the request. Then choose how long you want to share your location with that person.
- Tap **Cancel** if you do not wish to share your location.

You can also stop your friends from sending you new location sharing request.

- Tap **Me,** then toggle off **Allow Friend Requests.**

Request to See a Friend's Location

- Tap **People,** then click on the person whose location you wish to see, then tap **Ask to Follow Location.**

- Once the friend accepts your request, you can view their locations.

Remove a Friend

This action will remove the person from your People list and also remove you from their list.

- Tap **People,** then click on the person you wish to remove.
- Click on **Remove [name],** and then click on **Remove.**

See Your Friend's Location

- Tap **People,** then click on the person you wish to locate.
- Their location will show on the map if the friend can be located.
- If the friend can't be located, you will receive a **No Location Found** message under their name.

Contact a Friend

- Tap **People,** then click on the person you wish to contact.
- Tap **Contact** and then select how you intend to contact your friend.

Get Direction to a Friend

- Tap **People,** then click on the person.
- Tap **Directions** to launch the Map.
- Click on the friend's route to receive directions to your friend's current location.

Mark Favorite Friends

Friends you mark as a favorite will appear at the top of the People list.

- Tap **People,** then click on the person.

- Then click on **Add [name] to Favorites.** To remove the person from Favorites, tap **Remove [name] from Favorites.** Or
- Tap **People** and swipe left across the person's name, and then tap the star. To remove the person from Favorites, swipe left and tap the star.

Receive Notification when your friend Leaves or Arrives at a Location

- Tap **People,** then click on the person.
- Scroll to **Notifications,** tap **Add,** and then click on **Notify Me.**
- Choose the option that applies to you.
- Select a location or click on **New Location** to set up a new location and a location radius.
- Choose the number of times you want to receive the notification, tap **Add,** and then click on **OK.**

Change or Disable a Notification You Set

To change notification your friend receives about you or one that you receive about a friend,

- Tap **People,** then click on the person.
- Scroll to **Notifications,** tap the desired notification, then choose either of the options below:
1. To disable a notification, click on **Delete Notification,** then tap **Delete Notification** to complete.
2. To change a notification, enter the new details, then tap **Done.**

Choose who You Receive Location Updates from

Users with an Apple ID can notify you when they leave or arrive at a location. But you can select the persons that you want to receive location updates from.

- Tap **Me,** then click on **Receive Location Updates.**
- Then choose either **Everyone** or **People You Share with.**

Notify a Friend When Your Location Changes

- Tap **People,** then click on the person.
- Scroll to **Notifications,** tap **Add,** and then click on **Notify (Name).**
- Choose the option that applies to you.
- Select a location or click on **New Location** to set up a new location and a location radius.
- Choose the number of times you want your friend to receive the notification, and then tap **Add.**

See All Notifications about You

- Tap **Me,** then scroll to **Notifications about You** to view a list of the persons notified about changes in your location.
- Click on a name to view more details.

Turn off Notifications about You

You can switch off any location notification about you, both the ones you created and the ones that your friend created.

- Tap **Me,** then scroll to **Notifications about You** to view a list of the persons notified about changes in your location.
- Select a name and then click on a notification.
- Click on **Delete Notification,** then click on **Delete Notification.**

Add A Device to Find My

Before you can use the Find My app to locate a missing Apple device, you will need to connect the devices to your Apple ID. You can use one Apple device to find another Apple device. To add an iPad, iPhone, or iPod Touch,

- Go to Settings on your device and click on your name.
- Tap **Find My,** then click on **Find My (name of the device.)**
- Toggle on **Find My (name of the device),** and then toggle on the options below

    1. **Send Last Location:** When the missing device's battery level becomes critically low, the system will automatically send its location to Apple.

    2. **Find My network or Enable Offline Finding:** Find My will locate the missing device even if it is not connected to cellular or Wi-Fi.

To add a Mac

- Click on the Apple Menu on your Mac, then click on **System Preferences.**
- Then choose one of the options below:

    1. For macOS 10.15 and above, tap **Apple ID,** then click on **iCloud.**

    2. Tap **iCloud** for macOS 10.14 and below.

- Enter your Apple ID if prompted, click on **Find My Mac,** then tap **Allow.**

Find the Location of a Device

- Tap **Devices** in the Find My app, then click on the missing device.

- The device location will appear on the map. But if the device cannot be located, you will see the **No Location Found** message under the device's name.

Play a Sound on Your Missing Device

If you have your phone in the house, but can't seem to place where you left it, this option will make a sound on the missing device, helping you to find it faster. Do this with other Apple device using the same Apple ID

- Tap **Devices** in the Find My app, then click on the missing device.

- Tap **Play Sound,** and you will hear a sound after a short delay if the device is online. A Find My (device) alert will show on the missing device screen, and you will receive a confirmation email in your Apple ID email address.

- However, if the device is offline, you will see a **Sound Pending** message. The sound will go off once the device gets connected to cellular or Wi-Fi.

Stop Playing a Sound

Here is how to stop the sound from playing once you find your device.

- For Apple Watch, press the side button or the digital crown. You may also tap **Dismiss** on your screen.

- For iPhone, iPod Touch, or iPad, press the volume or power button or flip the Silent/ Ring switch. If the device is locked, first unlock it or swipe up to dismiss the Find My alert. For unlocked devices, tap **Ok** in the Find My alert.

- For Airpods, return the Airpods to their case and close the lid or click on **Stop** in the Find My app.
- For Mac, tap **OK** in the Find My Mac notification.

Get Directions to a Device

For directions to a device's current location,

- Click **Devices,** then click on the device you want.
- Tap **Directions** to launch Maps.
- Click on the route to receive direction to the device's location.

Mark a Device as Lost

See below how to enable **Lost Mode** on your device:

- Click **Devices,** then click on the device you want.
- Scroll to **Mark as Lost** and click on **Activate.**
- Then continue with the instructions on your screen.
- At the end of the setup, you will find **Activated** under the **Mark as Lost** part of your screen. However, if the device is not connected to cellular or Wi-Fi network when you marked it as lost, you will see **Pending** until the phone goes online again.

Change the Lost Mode Notification for a Lost Device

After you have marked your device as lost, you can modify your email notification or contact information settings:

- Click **Devices,** then click on the device you want.
- Scroll to **Mark as Lost** and click on **Activated** or **Pending.**

- Then do one of the following:
  - ✓ Modify the message or phone number if desired.
  - ✓ Toggle on **Receive Email Updates** if you want to get email updates.
- Tap **Done** to save.

Turn Off Lost Mode

To turn off lost mode when you find your missing device,

- Input the passcode for the device.
- Open **Find My** app, click on the device, and tap **Activated** or **Pending.**
- Tap **Turn Off Mark As Lost** and then click on **Turn Off.**

Erase a Device

To wipe off data from your missing device,

- Click **Devices,** then click on the device you want.
- Click on **Erase This Device**, then click on **Erase This (Device).**
- You may receive a prompt to enter a message or a phone number – indicating that the device is lost and how best to reach you. The message and number you provide will show on the lock screen of the missing device.
- Tap **Erase** and enter your Apple ID password.
- Then click on **Erase.**

Note: if the missing device is offline, the remote erase will only begin once the device connects to a Wi-Fi or cellular network.

Cancel an Erase

You can only cancel an erase request if the device was offline when you made the request, and you found it before it came online.

- Click on **Devices,** then click on the device you want.
- Tap **Cancel Erase** and enter your Apple ID password.

Remove a Device from Your Devices List

You can remove the device that you are not using from your devices list. If you enabled Activation Lock for that device, you would find the device in your devices list the next time the device comes online.

- Click on **Devices,** then click on the device.
- Tap **Remove This Device** and then click on **Remove.**

Remove Activation Lock on a Device You no Longer Have

Activation Lock helps to keep your Apple devices safe, in case it goes missing. With the activation lock enabled, another user will be unable to activate the device. If you gave your phone away, follow the steps below to disable activation lock:

- Click on **Devices,** then click on the device.
- Tap **Erase This Device** and then click on **Erase This (Device).**
- Do not input a message or phone number if the device isn't lost.
- Tap **Erase** and enter your Apple ID password.
- Then click on **Erase.** If the device is offline, the remote erase will begin when it connects to a cellular or Wi-Fi network. You will receive an email confirmation once the device is erased.
- With the device erased, click on **Remove this Device,** then click on **Remove.**

Chapter 6: Passcode on iPhone

Create passcode to give your phone better security. Another reason to set a passcode is to turn on data protection, which helps encrypt your phone data with 256-bit AES encryption.

Change or Set a Passcode

- Go to settings and tap **Face ID & Passcode.**
- Then click **Change Passcode** or **Turn Passcode.**
- Click **Passcode Options** to view available options for creating a password.

Change when iPhone Automatically Locks

- Go to Settings, tap **Display & Brightness.**
- Click **Auto-Lock** and choose the length of time.

Erase Data after Failed Passcodes

Configure your iPhone to erase your settings, media, and information once the wrong passcode is entered ten consecutive times.

- Go to settings and tap **Face ID & Passcode.**
- Then toggle on **Erase Data.**

Disable Passcode

- Go to settings and tap **Face ID & Passcode.**
- Then click **Turn Passcode Off.**

Chapter 7: Face ID on iPhone

Face ID allows you to conveniently and securely unlock your phone, authorize payments and purchases as well as sign into different third-party apps by merely staring at your phone.

Set Up Face ID

- Go to **Settings,** tap **Face ID & Passcode,** tap **Set up Face ID,** and proceed with the instructions on your screen.

You can also add an alternate appearance to the Face ID settings. Use the Alternate appearance to add another user or to add your face with accessories on.

- Go to **Settings,** tap **Face ID & Passcode,** tap **Set up an Alternate Appearance,** and proceed with the instructions on your screen.

Temporarily Disable Face ID

To temporarily prevent Face ID from unlocking your phone,

- Press and hold any of the volume buttons and the side button simultaneously for two seconds until the slider appears on your screen.

- Then press the side button to lock the iPhone instantly.

- The Face ID will be enabled again when next you unlock your phone with your passcode.

Disable Face ID

- Go to **Settings,** tap **Face ID & Passcode,** and then tap **Reset Face ID** to turn off Face ID.

- To disable Face ID for selected items, toggle off the option on your screen - **iPhone Unlock, iTunes & App Store, Apple Pay,** or **Safari AutoFill.**

Chapter 8: Widgets on the Home Screen

The Today View widget gathers all the current information from your favorite apps and displays them on your screen – details like calendar events, weather, today's headlines, and more. You can choose to have these widgets on your home screen to access this information quickly.

Open Today View

- Swipe right from the left edge of the Lock or Home screen to open Today View.

Move a Widget to the Home Screen

You can move widgets from Today View to your Home Screen with the steps below:

- Open Today View and search for the widget you want.
- Tap and hold the widget until it starts to jiggle, then drag it off the right side of your screen and place it in a position on the Home Screen.
- Tap **Done** to save.

Tip: you will find a widget with dots next to it; the widget is called a Smart Stack. It contains a set of widgets that use information like your location, the time, and activity to display the most relevant widget at different times in your day. You can add the widget to the Home Screen, then swipe through the stack to view the different widgets in it.

Add a Widget to a Home Screen Page

You can also add a widget to a home screen page

- Swipe to the Home Screen page where you want to keep the widget, then press down on the background until the apps start to jiggle.

- Click ✛ at the top of your screen to go to the widget gallery.

- Search for a widget, click it, and then swipe left to view the different size options. The different sizes display different details.

- When you get to the size that you want, click **Add Widget,** then click **Done.**

Edit a Widget

You can edit most widgets to show only the information you want – like customizing the Weather widget to show the forecast for a different area.

- Press down on a widget to open the Quick Actions menu.

- Tap **Edit Widget** or **Edit Stack** for a Smart Stack, then select the options you want. For instance, to change the location for a Weather widget, click **Location,** and then choose the desired location for the forecast.

  To edit a Smart Stack, you can enable or disable **Smart Rotate** and drag the ▤ icon to reorder the widgets.

- Tap the Home Screen to exit.

Remove a Widget from the Home Screen

- Press down on a widget to open the Quick Actions menu.

- Click **Remove Widget** or **Remove Stack,** then click **Remove.**

Access Today View on the Lock Screen

You can adjust the settings to allow access to Today View when your phone is locked:

- Go to Settings, tap **Face ID & Passcode.**
- Enter your passcode and toggle on **Today View.**

Chapter 9: Search with iPhone

Use 'Search on iPhone' to find apps and contacts, find and open webpages, search inside apps, and quickly start a web search.

To search,

- Swipe down from the middle of the Home Screen.
- Tap the search field and enter your search term. Tap **Go** on your keyboard to see all the search results.

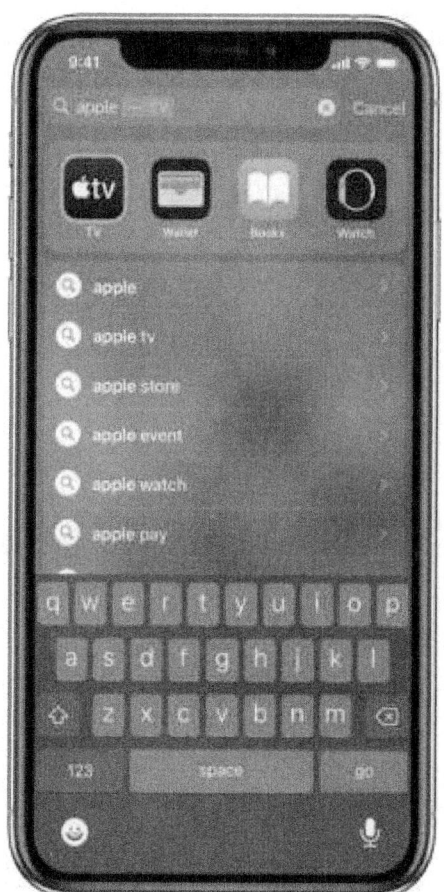

- Click on a suggested app to open it.

- To begin a new search, tap the $\otimes$ icon in the search field.

Search in Apps

Some apps have the search field or button to use in searching for something within the app.

- Click the search field or $\mathcal{Q}$ icon in an app, enter your search term, and tap **Search.**

Disable Siri Suggestions in Search

Siri studies your phone usage and offers suggestions based on collected data. This suggestion also appears in the search field. To turn it off,

- Go to Settings, tap **Siri & Search,** then disable **Suggestions in Search.**

Disable Location Services for Suggestions

To stop seeing suggestions based on your location,

- Go to Settings, tap **Privacy,** then click on **Location Services.**

- Tap **System Services** and disable **Location-Based Suggestions.**

Choose Apps to Include in Search

You can choose the apps that should show up in the search results.

- Go to Settings, and tap **Siri & Search.**

- Swipe down, click on an app, then turn **Show in Search** on or off.

Chapter 10: Control Center

The Control center grants users instant access to useful controls like screen brightness, Do not Disturb, airplane mode, etc.

Open Control Center

- Swipe down from the upper-right edge of your screen. Swipe up from the bottom to close the control center.

Add and Organize Controls

You can add more shortcuts and controls for several apps like Voice Memos, Notes, etc.

- Go to Settings, tap **Control Center,** tap or beside a control to remove or add the controls.

- To reorder the controls, touch beside a control and drag it to a different position.

Access More Controls in Control Center

Different controls in the control center have additional options. Touch and hold a control button to reveal the available options. For example,

- Touch and hold the icon to take a Photo, Take a Portrait or Take Selfie.

Touch and hold to
see Camera options.

Temporarily Disconnect from Wifi

- Open the Control Center and tap 📶 to disconnect from Wi-Fi. Tap it again to connect.

- Touch and hold 📶 to see the name of the network.

Turn off Wi-Fi

Disconnecting from Wi-Fi will not turn off wi-fi. To turn off,

- Go to Settings and tap **Wi-Fi.**

- To turn it on again, open the control center and tap ⛔.

Temporarily Disconnect from Bluetooth

- Open the Control Center and tap ⌗ to disconnect. Tap it again to connect.

To turn off Bluetooth,

- Go to Settings and tap **Bluetooth.**

- To turn it on again, open the control center and tap ⌗.

Disable Access to Control Center in Apps

To prevent your iPhone from accessing the control center while using apps,

- Go to **Settings,** tap **Control Center,** and disable **Access Within Apps.**

Chapter 11: Screenshots

Take a Screenshot

- Press and release the volume up and side buttons simultaneously.

- Click the screenshot at the lower-left part of your screen and tap **Done.**

- Then tap either **Save to Files, Save to Photos** or **Delete Screenshot.**

Tip: you can quickly create a PDF of an email, document, or webpage.

- Take a screenshot, click the screenshot thumbnail at the bottom left of your screen, then click **Full Page** to screenshot the rest of the screen.

Screen Recording

See the steps below on how to record your screen and include sound in your recording.

- Go to **Settings,** tap **Control Center,** and tap ⊕ beside **Screen Recording.**

- Open the Control Center, tap 🔘, hold for the three-second countdown, and then begin recording your screen.

- To stop screen recording, open the control center, tap the ⊙ icon, and then tap **Stop.**

- To include audio or sound in your recording, press deeply on the ⊙ icon and then click **Microphone.**

- Go to the Photos app to view your screen recording.

Chapter 12: Home Screen and App Library

You can find your apps on the Home screen and the App Library. You can also choose to have most of your apps on the App Library and delete the Home screen pages.

Open Apps on Home Screen

- Swipe up from your screen's bottom edge to go home.

- Swipe left or right to view all the apps on the Home screen pages.

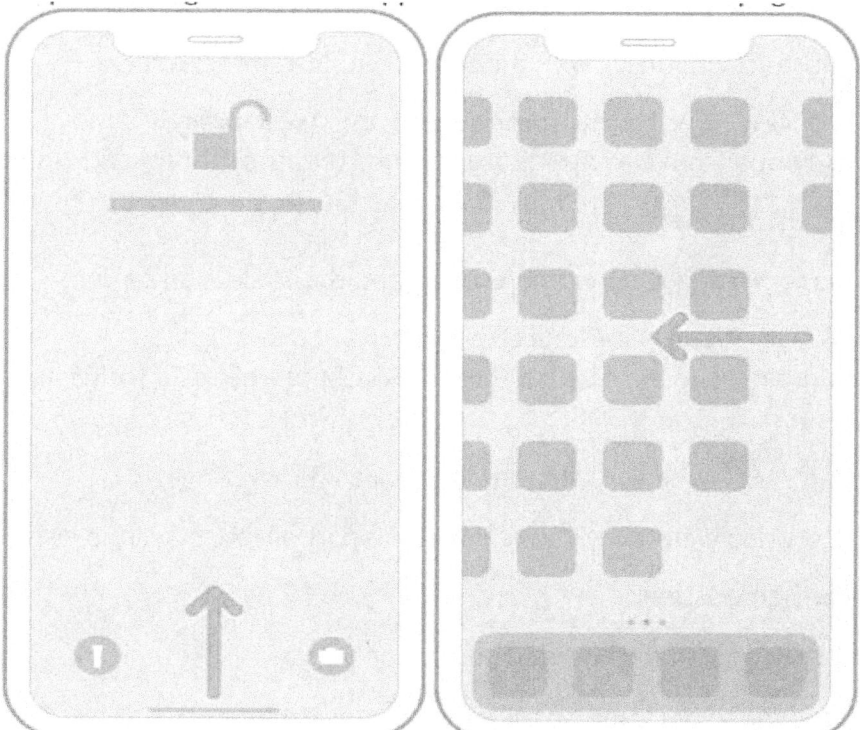

- Click on an app icon to open the app.

- Swipe up from your screen's bottom edge to return to the first page of the Home screen.

Explore the App Library

By default, the App Library breaks the apps into categories like Entertainment, Creativity, and so on. The apps you use frequently appear near the top of your screen. To go to the App Library,

- Return to the Home screen, and swipe left past all the home screen pages. Tap an app to open it.

- Use the search field at the top of the screen to search for apps.

- To add an app to the home screen, tap and hold the app to open the quick actions menu, then select **Add to Home Screen.**

Download New Apps to the Home Screen and App Library

Download apps from the App store to both the App Library and Home Screen or just the App library.

- Go to Settings, tap **Home Screen,** and then select an option.

Multitask with Picture-in-Picture

This feature allows you to watch a video or FaceTime while using other apps.

- Tap when watching a video or FaceTiming.

- The video window will scale down to a part of your screen to display the home screen.

- Tap an app on the home screen to open it.

- Pinch open or closed on the video window to resize it.

- Click the video window to display the controls.

- Drag the window to put it in a different area.

- To hide the video window, drag it off the right or left edge of your screen. Tap to close the video window.

- Tap  in the video window to return to full screen.

Switch Between Apps on iPhone

Use the App Switcher to move from one app to another quickly.

- Swipe up from the bottom edge of your screen and pause in the center of the screen to open the App Switcher.

- Swipe through the apps and click on an app to open it.

Move Apps Around the Home Screen

Move apps from the home screen into the dock/ other Home screen pages.

- Tap and hold an app on the Home screen, then select **Edit Home Screen.**
- Then drag the app to another home screen page, the dock at the bottom of the screen, or another position on the same page. To move it to a new page, drag it to the right edge, then wait for some seconds for the new page to show.

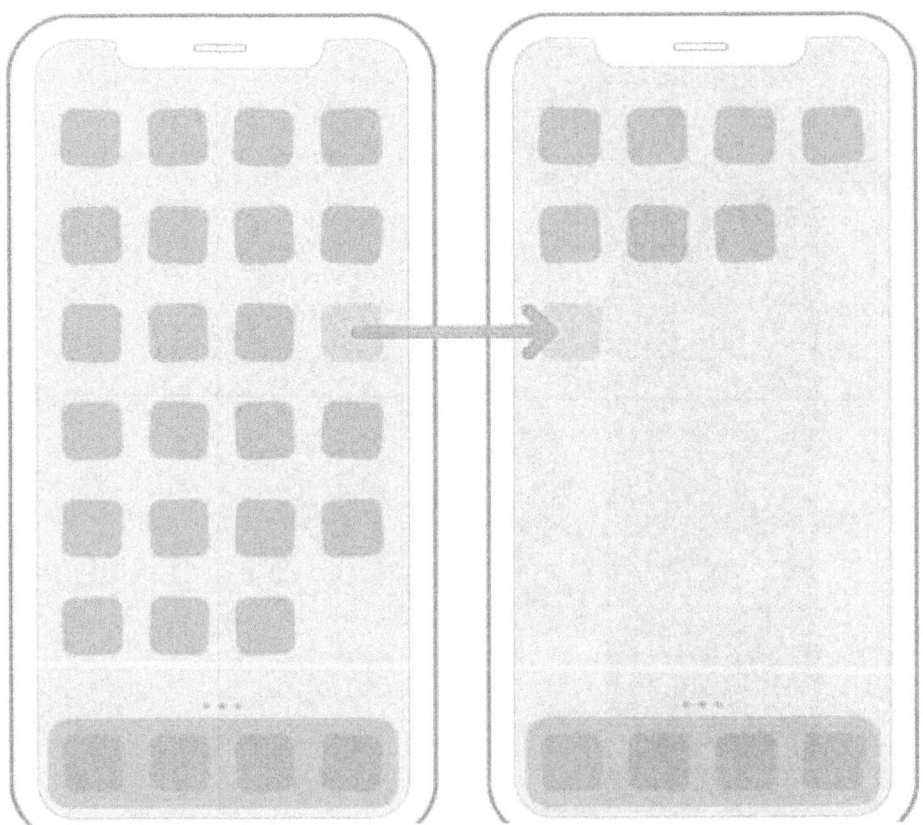

- Tap **Done** to finish.

Create Folders
Add your apps to folders to make them easy to find.

- Tap and hold an app on the Home screen, then select **Edit Home Screen.**

- Drag one app onto another to create a folder, then drag other apps into the folder.

- Click on the name field to rename the folder. Tap **Done** to finish.

- Drag all the apps out of a folder to delete the folder.

Reset the Home Screen Layout

To return apps to their original layout,

- Go to Settings, tap **General,** then click **Reset.**

- Then select **Reset Home Screen Layout** to finish – this will remove any folder you created and order the apps alphabetically.

Quit and Repen Apps

Quit and reopen an app that is not working properly.

- To quit an app, open the App switcher, swipe to the app, then swipe up on the app.

- Then tap the app on the App library or home screen to open it.

Remove Apps from Home Screen

- Tap and hold an app on the home screen to open the quick actions menu.

- Click **Remove App,** then select **Delete App** to delete the app from your iPhone or select **Move to App Library** to keep the app in the App Library.

Delete an App

- Tap and hold the app, select **Delete App,** then click **Delete.**

- The app will be deleted from the App Library and Home Screen.

Chapter 13: FaceTime

Use the FaceTime app to make audio or video calls to your friends and family, whether they have an iPad, iPhone, or a Mac. You can use the front camera to talk face-to-face and the rear camera to show your surrounding

Set Up FaceTime

- Go to **Settings,** tap **FaceTime,** and then enable **FaceTime.**
- Turn on **FaceTime Live Photos** to take Live Photos during FaceTime calls.
- Input your Apple ID, email address, or phone number you want to use with FaceTime.

Make a FaceTime Call

- Open the FaceTime app and tap ✛ at the upper right of your screen.
- Enter the number or name of the person you want to call in the entry field at the top, then tap **Audio** 📞 for an audio call or **Video** 🎥 for video call.
- If no one answers your call, click on **Leave a Message** to drop a message, **Cancel** to end the call, or **Call Back** to attempt calling back.
- Tap ⊗ to leave an active call at any time.

To call someone you called previously from your FaceTime call history,

- Click the number or name in the history tab, or tap (i) to choose a number or name in **Contacts** and make your call from there.

Receive FaceTime Call

When you have an incoming FaceTime call,

- Tap **Accept** to take the call or **Decline** to reject the call.

- Tap **Message** to send a message to the caller or **Remind Me** to create a reminder to call back.

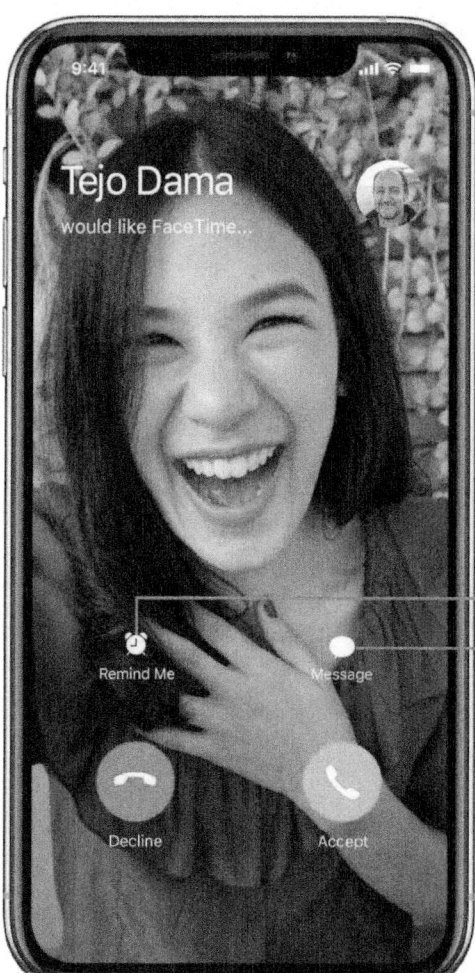

Set up a reminder to return the call later.

Send the caller a text message.

- If the call comes in while you are on another call, you may tap **Hold & Accept** or **End & Accept** to take the new call.

Start a FaceTime Call from a Message Conversation

See how to start a FaceTime call with someone you are chatting with.

- Open a message conversation, click or the person's profile picture or name at the top, then tap **FaceTime.**

If you want to make a Group FaceTime call with all the group members, tap the profile pictures and tap **FaceTime** in a group message conversation.

Delete a Call from Your Call History

- Open FaceTime, and swipe left on a call in your call history, then click **Delete.**

Start a Group FaceTime Call

- Tap at the upper right of your screen.
- Enter the numbers or names of the people you want to call in the entry field at the top, then tap **Audio** for an audio call or **Video** for video call. To choose people from your contacts, tap .
- If no one answers your call, click on **Leave a Message** to drop a message, **Cancel** to end the call, or **Call Back** to attempt calling back.

- Tap to leave an active group call at any time.

Customize the FaceTime Tile for Group Call

By default, the tile for the person speaking is larger than that of other people on the call. To change this setting,

- Go to Settings, tap **FaceTime,** scroll to **Automatic Prominence,** and disable **Speaking.**

- This will make every participant have equal tile on your screen.

Add Another Person to a Call

Anyone can add other people during a Group FaceTime call:

- While a group call is ongoing, click on your screen to show the controls, then swipe up from the top of the controls and click **Add Person.**

- Enter the phone number, name, or Apple ID of the person, or tap to choose from your contacts.

- Then click **Add Person to FaceTime.**

Take Live Photo in FaceTime

Before you can take FaceTime Live Photo, you need to check that the option is turned on.

- Go to **Settings,** tap **FaceTime,** and then enable **FaceTime Live Photos.**

To take Live Photo,

- Tap on a call with one person.

- On a Group FaceTime call, click the tile of the person you want, tap then click.

- Both parties will receive a notification that you took a Live Photo.

Use Other Apps during FaceTime Call

You can still access other apps while making a FaceTime call.

- Swipe up from your screen's bottom edge to go to the home screen.

- Click an app icon to open the app.

- Tap the FaceTime icon or the green bar at the top of your screen to return to the FaceTime screen.

Become a Memoji

You can create a Memoji character and use it for your FaceTime calls. The character imitates all your movement, voice, and facial expression.

- While making a FaceTime call, tap your screen and then tap.

- Click , swipe through the characters at the bottom, and then click on the one you like.

- The other caller will hear you but will see your Memoji doing the talking.

Add Filter to Your Appearance

Add filters to your face during a FaceTime call:

- While making a FaceTime call, tap your screen and then tap.

- Tap and tap a filter at the bottom to use it.

Add Text Labels and Shapes

To add a text label to your screen during a call,

- Tap ⊛ , select **Aa** , then click a text label. Swipe up from the top of the text window to view more label options.

- After selecting a label, enter text, then click outside the text.

- Position the label on any part of your screen.

- To delete the label, click on it, then tap ⊗ .

To add shapes,

- Tap ⊛ , tap 〰 and choose a shape.

- Then pull it to a location that you want, or tap the shape, and tap ⊗ to delete it.

Add Memoji Stickers

- While making a FaceTime call, tap your screen and then tap ⊛ .

- Tap ⊛ to add an Emoji sticker or ⊛ to add a Memoji sticker. You may also tap **Aa** , swipe up and select ☺ for a smiley sticker.

- Click on a sticker to use it on the call, then pull it to a location that you want.

- Or, tap the sticker, and then tap ⊗ to delete the sticker.

Change FaceTime Video and Audio Settings

While on a FaceTime call, tap your screen to show the controls, and then use any of the options below:

- Tap 🎤 to turn off the sound.

- Tap 🔄 to switch between rear and front camera.

- To put off your camera, swipe up from the top of the controls, then click **Camera Off.** Click it again to turn the camera on.

Switch from FaceTime Call to Message Conversation

While on a FaceTime call, you can move from the call to Messages,

- Click on your screen to view the controls, swipe up from the top

  of the controls, and then click ⬤ .

Block Unwanted Callers in FaceTime

You can block people from sending you messages, calling, or videoing you on FaceTime.

- Go to Settings, tap **Face Time,** and then tap **Blocked Contacts.**

- Scroll down and click **Add New,** then choose the contacts you want to block.

- To unblock, swipe left on the contact, then tap **Unblock.**

Chapter 14: Apple Pay

Apple Pay is simpler and safer than using your physical cards. Use Apple Pay to make purchases on websites, apps, and stores that support Apple Pay. You can also send and receive money from family and friends.

Set Up Apple Pay

The first step is to add your cards to your Wallet

- Open the Wallet app and tap ⊕. You may be prompted to sign in with your Apple ID.

- To add new cards, enter the card details manually or use your phone camera to capture the card details.

- To add previous cards, choose the cards you removed, cards set up on Apple Pay on your other devices, or the cards linked with your Apple ID. Tap **Continue** and input the CVV number for the selected cards

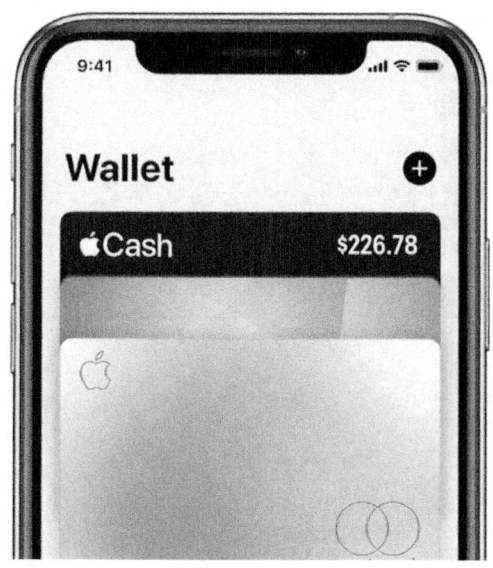

Choose Default Card

The Wallet app uses the first card you add as your default card. To choose a different default card,

- Open the Wallet app and locate the card that should be your default card.
- Touch and hold the card, then pull it to the front of the stack.
- The card that is in the front of the stack is automatically your default card.

Pay with your Default Card

- Tap the side button two times to bring up your default card, stare at your phone, or enter your passcode to authenticate.
- Then place the top of your phone within a few centimeters of the contactless reader. Wait till you see **Done** and a checkmark on your screen.

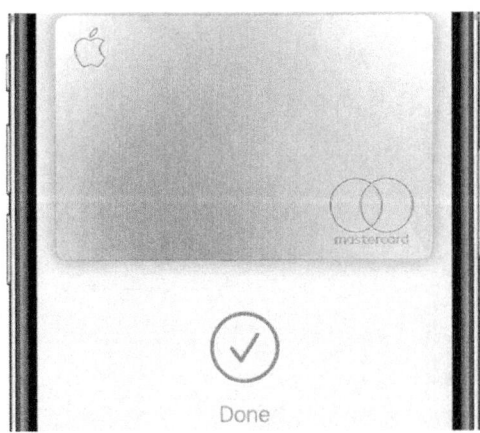

Pay with a Different Card

If you prefer using another card other than your default card,

- Press the side button two times to bring up the default card. Click on the default card and then choose a different card.

- Authenticate with Face ID or passcode.

- Then place the top of your phone within a few centimeters of the contactless reader. Wait till you see **Done** and a checkmark.

Pay in an App, on the Web or App Clip

- During checkout, click the **Apple Pay** button.

- Read the payment information, tap the side button two times, and stare at your phone to authenticate with Face ID.

- You may also choose to authenticate using your passcode.

Update Your Contact & Shipping Information

See the steps below on how to update your contact and shipping details.

- Go to **Settings,** tap **Wallet & Apple Pay,** and then change any option on your screen – Email, phone, or shipping address.

Shop on Your Mac and Pay on Your iPhone

You can start the transaction on your Mac and complete payment on your iPhone. You need to turn on Bluetooth on the two devices. The devices also have to be near each other, have an active internet connection, and are connected to the same Apple ID.

- Begin checkout on your Mac, tap the Apple Pay button, and review the payment information.

- Then tap the side button on your iPhone two times, and authenticate with your Face ID.

- You can disable this option if you do not want to use the Apple Pay app on your phone to complete payments initiated on your Mac.

- Go to **Settings,** tap **Wallet & Apple Pay,** and then disable **Allow Payments on Mac.**

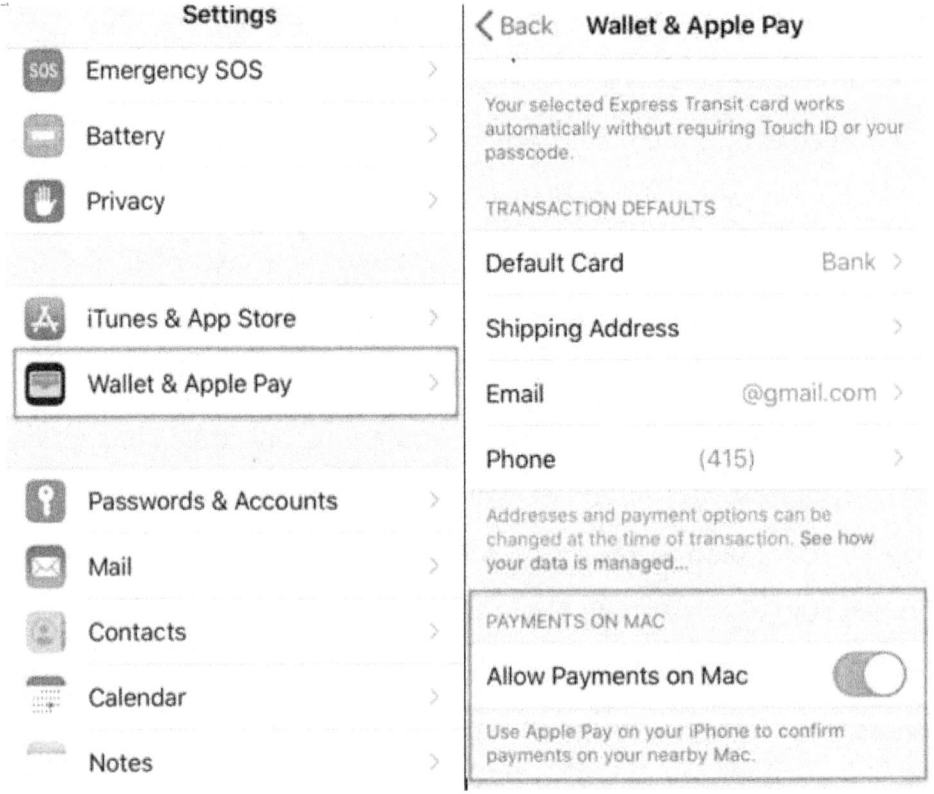

Update Card Details or Delete Card

- Go to **Settings,** tap **Wallet & Apple Pay,** click on a card, and then click the information you want to change, like the billing address.

- To delete the card, tap **Remove this Card** at the end of your screen. Or open the Wallet app, click on a card, tap ⬤then tap **Remove this Card** at the end of your screen.

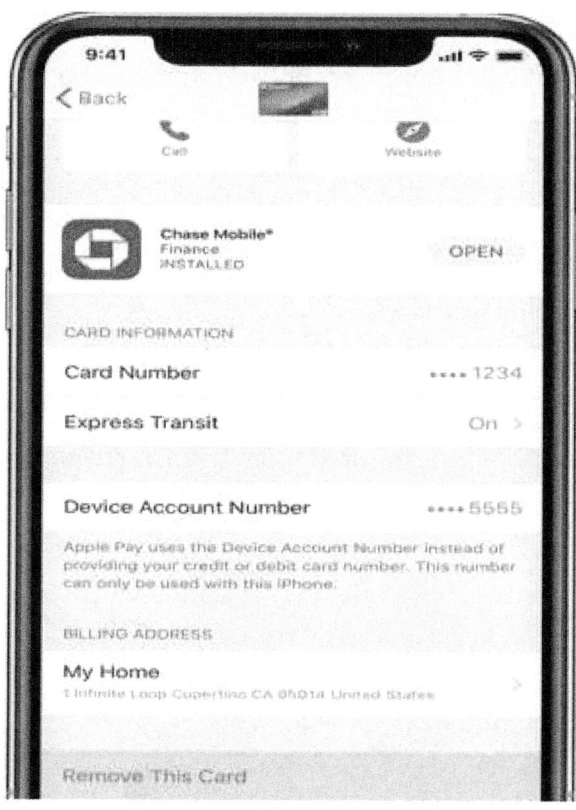

Change Apple Pay Settings

- Go to **Settings,** tap **Wallet & Apple Pay,** and then customize settings on your screen.

- Toggle on or off **Double-Click Side Button** to bring up your cards whenever you press the side button.

Set Up Apple Cash

When someone sends you money via the Message app, the money is added to your Apple Cash card. You can then spend the money from the Apple cash balance or send it to your bank account.

- Go to **Settings,** tap **Wallet & Apple Pay,** and then enable **Apple Cash.**

Manage Apple Cash

- Open the Wallet app and select the Apple Cash card.
- Scroll down to view your transactions.
- Tap and then choose an option on your screen to request a statement, update your bank account details, transfer money, etc.

Send Payment in Messages

- Open the Messages app and click on an iMessage conversation.
- Tap and choose an amount.
- Tap **Pay,** enter a comment if you like, and then click .
- Review the payment information, and then authenticate with a passcode or Face ID.

You can only cancel a payment if the receiver is yet to accept it. Click the payment bubble and select **Cancel Payment.**

Note: if you do not see the button, tap the button first and then tap the Pay button.

Request Payment

- Open the iMessage conversation, tap  and choose an amount.

- Tap **Request,** and send your payment request.

Apply for Apple Card

Apple Card is an Apple Credit card for eligible Apple users. To apply for the card,

- Open the Wallet app, tap , then click **Apply for Apple Card.**

- Input the requested details and agree to the terms and conditions to submit your application.

- When your application is approved, you will see the initial credit limit and APR. Click **Accept Apple Card** to accept the card or click **No Thanks** to refuse.

Use Apple Card

You can use the Apple Card in locations that do not accept Apple Pay. However, you will need to request for the physical card to use the card in stores. To use the card over the phone, on the web, or in apps,

- Open the Wallet app & tap **Apple Card.**

- Tap , then click **Card Information** to view the card security code, card number, and expiration date.

To view your Apple Card transactions and statement,

- Open the Wallet app & tap **Apple Card.**

- Scroll down to view your transactions or tap **Weekly Activity** to view your spending in the current week. Tap **View Monthly** to get a monthly summary.

- Click **Card Balance** to view new spendings, last month's balance, credits, and debits.

Make Payments with Apple Card

- Open the Wallet app, tap **Apple Card,** and then tap .

- For scheduled payments, select **Pay Different Amount** or **Pay My Bill,** input the payment details and then authenticate with a passcode or Face ID.

- To make a payment, pull the checkmark in the circle image to increase or reduce the payment amount or click Show Keypad to input an amount manually. Tap **Pay Later** or **Pay Now,** review the payment information, and then authenticate with a passcode or Face ID.

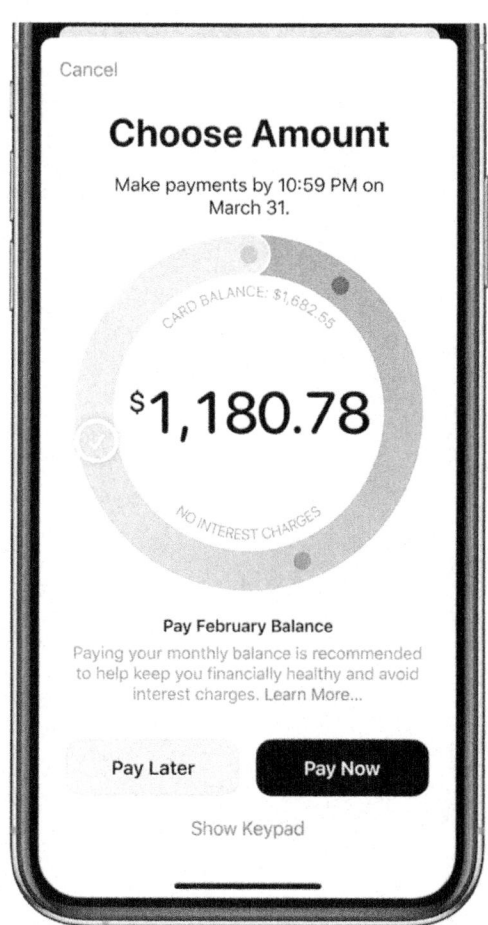

Remove Your Cards from Apple Pay if your Device is Stolen or Lost

You can do any of the following to remove your cards from Apple Pay on a missing device:

- Go to https://appleid.apple.com/#!&page=signin on your Mac or PC and sign in with your Apple ID. Tap the missing device in the **Devices** section, and tap **Remove All** below the list of cards.

- If you have another iPhone, iPod Touch, or iPad, go to Settings, tap your name, tap the missing phone, and click **Remove All Cards.**

- **Call your card issuers.**

Chapter 15: iMessage

With the Messages app , you can send text messages as SMS/ MMS messages to everyone or send iMessage to people who use Apple devices. You can send videos, photos, and other info as iMessage texts. When others are typing, you can see and send read receipts to let the sender know that you have read their messages. SMS/ MMS texts show in green bubbles and blue bubbles for iMessage texts.

Sign in to iMessage

- Go to Settings, tap **Messages,** then turn on **iMessage.**

Use Messages in iCloud

Activate Messages on iCloud to sync your messages across all your devices that have Messages in iCloud turned on.

- Go to Settings, tap your name, tap iCloud, then turn on **Messages.**

Send a Message

- Open the Messages app and tap at the upper right of your screen to start a new message. Or click on an existing conversation.

- If creating a new conversation, enter the contact name, Apple ID, or phone number of each recipient or tap to choose from your contact list.

- If using a dual SIM and want to send it from a different line, click on the line showing on your screen, then select the second line.

- Enter your message in the text field and then click to send.

97

- You will see the ⓘ icon if the message wasn't sent. Click the alert to resend the message.

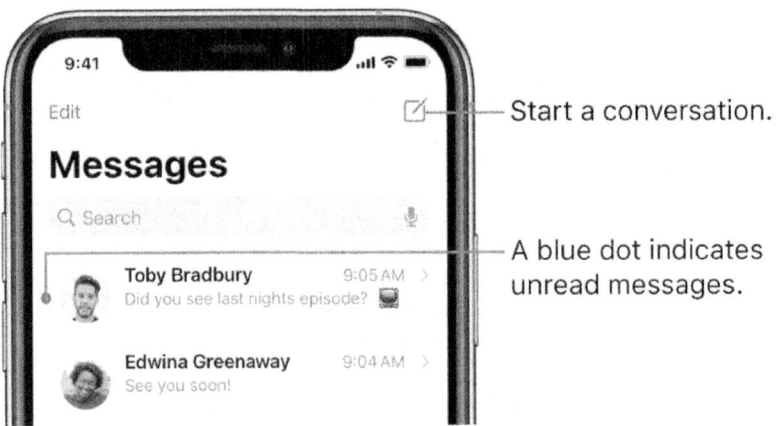

Start a conversation.

A blue dot indicates unread messages.

Tip: drag the message bubble to the left to view the time the message was received or sent.

Reply to a Message

- Click on the message you want to respond to, enter your response in the text field.

- Tap 🌐 or 😃 to replace the text with emoji.

- Click ⬆ to send your message.

Share Your Name and Photo

iOS 14 allows you to share your name and photo when you respond or start a new message. You can use a custom image or a Memoji as your photo and share it with anyone using iMessage. You can also turn sharing on or off.

- Open Messages, tap ••• and then click on **Edit Name and Photo.**

- Click on the text field where the name appears to change your name.

- Toggle on the switch for **Name and Photo Sharing** to share your name and photo.

- Choose an option under **Share Automatically** to set who can see your profile photo and name.

- To choose a profile picture, tap **Edit** close to the top of your screen and then choose your photo, Memoji, emoji, or image.

- Tap **Done** to save.

Pin or Unpin a Conversation

Pin selected conversations to the top of the Messages screen, so the individuals you contact frequently comes first in the list. To Pin,

- Swipe right on a conversation and then click 📌.

- Or press down on a conversation and drag it to the top of the list.

To unpin,

- Press down on a pinned conversation, then tap 📌.

- Or press down on a conversation and pull it to the bottom of the message list.

Reply to a Specific Message in a Conversation

If you have several messages in a conversation, follow the steps below to respond to a specific message.

- Open the conversation and double-click a message.

- Tap ↰ , write your response, and then click ⬆ .

Mention People in a Conversation

While in a group conversation, you can mention people to draw their attention to the message.

- Start typing the name of the contact in the text field, then select the name once it shows up on your screen.

- Proceed with your message and then click ⬆ .

- Another way to mention a contact is to type @ followed by the name of the contact.

You can also modify your notification settings for when you have a mention in Messages,

- Go to Settings, tap **Message,** and then click **Notify Me.**

Change Group Name and Photo

- Open the group conversation, tap the number or name at the top of your screen.

- Tap at the upper right, tap **Change Name and Photo,** then select an option.

Send a Video or Photo

- While writing a new message, tap to take a photo, frame the shot in the viewfinder, and then click .

- Tap to take a video, swipe to **Video** mode, then click .

- To choose a video or photo from your gallery, click in the app drawer, then scroll through your recent shots or click **All Photos** to view your complete gallery. Click a photo to select it.

- Write your message, if any, tap to send or to cancel.

Edit or Mark-Up a Photo

You can edit or write on a photo before you send it.

- While writing your message, tap close to the bottom and choose a photo.

- Click the photo, tap **Edit** and use the photo editing tools on your screen to edit the photo, then click **Done.**

- Click **Markup,** use the Markup tools on your screen to draw on the photo and then click **Done.**

101

- Tap **Done,** write your message and tap  to send or to delete the photo from the message bubble.

Send an Audio Message

Follow the steps below to send an audio message rather than text:

- Open a new or existing message, press down the icon to record an audio message.

- Click ⓟ to play your message before you send, tap 🔼 to send, or ⊗ to cancel.

To listen or reply to an audio message,

- Raise your phone to your ear to play the incoming audio messages, then raise your phone again to reply.

To turn off the 'Raise to Listen' feature,

- Go to Settings, tap **Messages,** then disable **Raise to Listen.**

iPhone deletes your audio messages two minutes after you play them, except you click **Keep.** But you can choose not to delete your audio messages:

- Go to Settings, tap **Messages,** tap **Expire,** and then click **Never.**

Send a Handwritten Message

Write your message using your finger, and the receiver will see the message just as if you used ink on paper.

- Open a conversation and rotate your phone to landscape orientation.

- Click 𝒐 on your keyboard, select a saved message at the bottom of your screen or use your finger to write a message, then tap **Done.**

- Click 🔼 to send your message or ⊗ to cancel.

- Any new message you write will be saved at the bottom of the handwriting screen. Click on the saved message to use it again. To delete a saved message, press down on the message until it jiggles, then tap ⊗.

Scroll to write a longer message.

Choose a saved message.
Touch and hold to delete
a saved message.

Return to the
keyboard.

Manage Your Messages or Attachment

To print, share, copy, save or delete an attachment or message,

- To copy an attachment in a conversation, open the conversation, press down on the attachment, and tap **Copy.**

- To print, save or share the attachment, tap the attachment, and then click ⬆️.

- To delete the attachment/ message, press down on the attachment or message, tap **More** to choose more messages, then tap 🗑️.

- To forward an attachment or message, press down on the attachment or message, tap **More** to choose more messages, then tap ⤵ .

Download and Use iMessage Apps

iMessage apps allow you to collaborate with others in a conversation, share a song, decorate messages with stickers, etc., without leaving Messages. To download,

- Open a Message conversation, and click 🅰 to go to the iMessage App Store.

- Click an app to view more details, then tap GET to download free apps or tap the price for Paid apps.

- To use the downloaded iMessage app, open a conversation in Messages, and tap the iMessage app in the app drawer.

- Click an item in the app to include it to a message bubble.

- Write your message, then click ⬆ to send your message or ⊗ to cancel.

Manage iMessage Apps

- Open a Message conversation and tap ••• in the app drawer.

- Click **Edit** and drag ≡ beside an app to reorder the app.

- Tap ⊕ beside an iMessage app to add it to your favorites, or ⊖ to remove the app from your Favorites.

- Turn off an iMessage app that you want to hide.

- Swipe left on an app to delete it, then tap **Delete.**

Create Your Own Memoji

- Open a conversation, tap  and then click  .

- Click each feature and select the options you want. Then click **Done** to add the Memoji.

- To duplicate, edit, or delete the Memoji, tap , click the Memoji, tap  and choose your option.

Send Memoji and Memoji Stickers

The Messages app automatically creates sticker packs using the Memoji and Memoji characters on your device. To use the stickers,

106

- Open a conversation, tap and then click a Memoji to view the available stickers.

- Click a sticker to add it to your message, enter a message if desired, and then click to send.

Send Memoji Recordings or Animated Memoji

You can send your friends Memoji messages that mimic your voice ad facial expressions.

- Open a conversation, tap and then select a Memoji.

- Click to record your voice and facial expressions, then tap the red square icon to stop the recording.

- Tap **Replay** to see the message before you send it.

- Click to send your message or to cancel.

Chapter 16: AirDrop

AirDrop allows you to wirelessly send your location, websites, videos, photos, etc. to other devices and Mac computers nearby.

Share an Item using AirDrop

- Open the content you want to share, click **Share,** or the ⬆️ icon. If sharing from the Photos app, swipe left and right to select more images.

- Tap the 🛜 icon in the row of share options, then click the profile picture of the nearby AirDrop user.

Tip: Point your phone towards another iPhone 12, then click the profile picture of the iPhone 12 user at the top of the screen.

- If you can't find the nearby AirDrop user, ask them to open the control center on their device, and allow AirDrop to receive items. Ask a Mac user to go to Finder and allow themselves to be discovered in AirDrop.

Allow Others Send items to You Using AirDrop

To allow your device to be found and to accept items from other users,

- Open the control center and tap 🛜.

- If you can't find the 🛜 icon, tap, and hold the top-left group of controls.

- Select either **Everyone** or **Contacts Only** to select the persons that can send to you using AirDrop.

Chapter 17: Siri

Siri, Apple's Virtual Assistant, is one quick way to get things done on your phone. You can ask Siri to set a timer, report on the weather, translate a phrase, and lots more.

Set Up Siri

- Go to Settings on your phone and click on **Siri & Search.**
- Then turn on **Listen for "Hey Siri"** if you like to summon Siri with your voice.
- To summon Siri with a button, turn on **Press Side Button for Siri.**

Summon Siri with your Voice

When you use audio commands to summon Siri, Siri will also respond with verbal cues.

- Begin with "Hey Siri," followed by the task or question you want.
- To ask another question or perform another task, tap or say **Hey Siri** again.

Summon Siri with a Button

When you use the button commands to summon Siri, Siri will respond silently if your phone is in silent mode or loudly if the phone is in ring mode.

- Tap and hold the side button.
- Once Siri appears on your screen, you may proceed to make a request or ask a question.

- To ask another question or perform another task, tap .

Make Your Request Clearly

If Siri misunderstands you,

- Tap and then rephrase your request, or spell out part of your request.

- You can also edit your request with text if the request is displayed on your screen – click on it, then use the on-screen keyboard to edit.

Type to Siri

You can type your request to Siri rather than speaking. Follow the steps below to turn on the feature:

- Go to Settings on your phone and click on **Accessibility.**

- Tap **Siri,** then toggle on **Type to Siri.**

- To make a request or ask a question, first summon Siri, then enter your question or task in the text field on your screen.

Tell Siri who You are

You need to complete the **My Cards** information in the Contacts app, then do the following:

- Go to Settings on your phone and click on **Siri & Search.**

- Tap **My Information,** and then click on your name.

Change when Siri Responds

Use settings below to configure when you want Siri to respond.

- Go to Settings on your phone and click on **Siri & Search.** Then choose any of the following:

- Disable **Listen for "Hey Siri"** to stop Siri from responding to your voice commands.

- Disable **Press Side Button for Siri** to stop Siri from responding to the side button clicks.

- Disable **Allow Siri when Locked** to stop access to Siri when your phone screen is locked.

- To change the Language Siri can respond to, click on **Language,** and choose the new language.

Change How Siri Responds

Configure how you want to receive feedback from Siri

- Go to Settings, click on **Siri & Search,** and then choose any of the following:

- To change the voice for Siri, click on **Siri Voice** and then change the accent or choose either a female or a male voice for Siri.

- To change when you want Siri to provide a voice response, click on **Siri Responses,** scroll to **Spoken Responses,** and choose your preference.

- If you want Siri's response to always show on your screen, click on **Siri Responses,** then enable **Always Show Siri Captions.**

- To view your request on your screen, click on **Siri Responses,** then enable **Always Show Speech.**

Hide Apps when you Summon Siri

You can choose to make your active apps invisible when you summon Siri.

- Go to Settings on your phone and click on **Accessibility.**
- Tap **Siri,** then toggle off **Show Apps Behind Siri.**

Change Where the Siri Suggestions Appear

You can turn on or off Siri's suggestions from different parts of your screen.

- Go to Settings on your phone and click on **Siri & Search.** Then disable or enable any of the following:
  - ✓ Suggestions on Home Screen
  - ✓ Suggestions while Searching
  - ✓ Suggestions when Sharing
  - ✓ Suggestions on Lock Screen

Modify Siri Settings for an Individual App

You can change the Siri shortcuts or Siri Suggestions settings for a single app.

- Go to Settings and click on **Siri & Search.**
- Click on an app and modify it as you please.

Adjust Siri Voice Volume

To increase or reduce the Siri voice volume, simply use the volume buttons or ask Siri to either "Turn down the volume" or "Turn up the volume."

Retrain Siri with your Voice

To train Siri again to know your voice,

- Go to Settings on your phone and click on **Siri & Search.**

- Disable **Listen for "Hey Siri,"** then turn it on again.

Control Voice Feedback for Siri

To choose when you want Siri to respond

- Go to Settings and click on **Accessibility.**

- Tap **Siri,** then choose from the options on your screen: **Only Speak with Hey Siri, Don't Speak in Silent Mode,** or **Always Speak Responses.**

Disable Hey Siri when your Phone is Facing Down

You can stop your phone from listening for the Siri's voice summon when your phone is facing down or covered.

- Go to Settings and click on **Accessibility.**

- Tap **Siri,** then disable **Always Listen for "Hey Siri."**

Chapter 18: Mail App

Use the Mail app ✉ to write and edit emails, receive and send photos, documents, drawings, videos, etc.

Create an Email Message

- Open the Mail app and tap ▢ at the bottom of your screen.
- If you have multiple email accounts, tap the **From** field, and then choose an email account.
- Enter the receiver's email address in the **To** field. You may also enter an email address in the **CC** and **BCC** fields. As you type, the Mail app will automatically suggest people saved on your Contacts. You may tap ⊕ icon to open the Contacts app and choose your recipients from there. Use the BCC field to enter the email address of persons whose names you do not want other receivers to see.
- Enter your subject in the subject field and enter your message in the message field.
- Tap the ↑ button at the top right side of your screen to send your email.

Change mailboxes
or accounts.

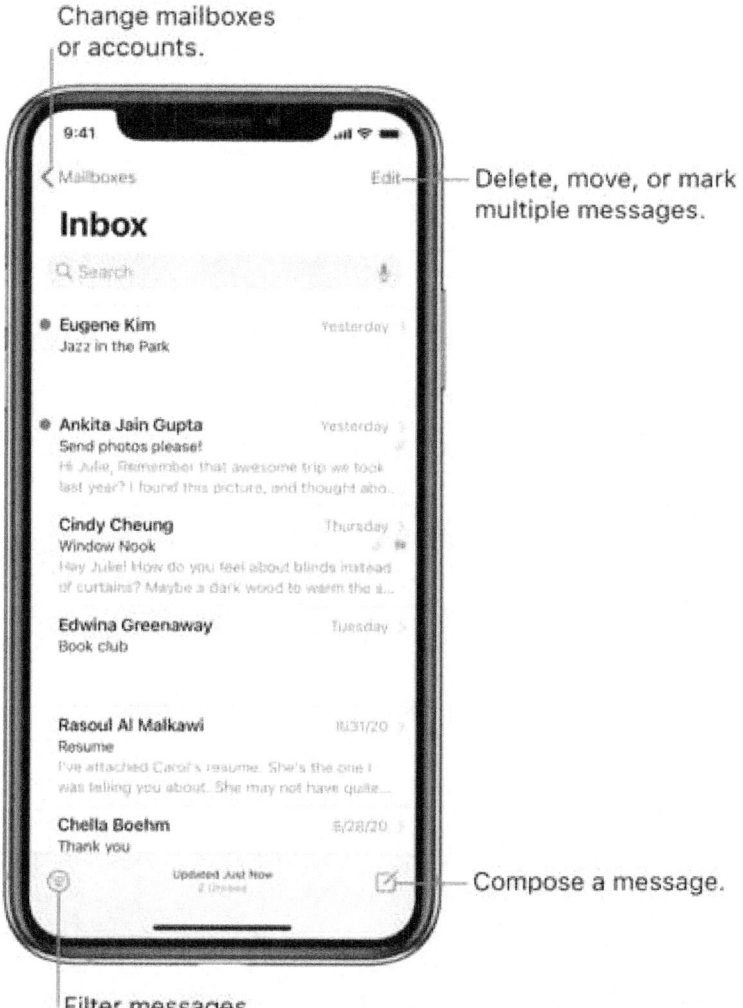

Delete, move, or mark
multiple messages.

Compose a message.

Filter messages.

Reply to an email

- Open the email app, click on an email, tap the button.

- Tap **Reply,** enter your response and then tap the button at the top right side of your screen to send your email.

You can quote some text in the sender's email while drafting your response. To do this,

- Open the email you want to reply to, tap and hold the first word of the text you want to quote, then drag your finger to the last word to select it, then tap the ⬑ button.

- Tap **Reply,** enter your response, and then tap the ⬆ button at the top right side of your screen to send your email.

To disable indentation of quoted texts,

- Go to the Settings app ⚙ and click on **Mail.**
- Then tap **Increase Quote Level.**

Attach Document, Photo, or Video to an Email

To attach a saved document, photo, or video,

- Start typing or responding to an email, then tap the ‹ icon in the format bar above the keyboard.

- To insert a video or photo, tap the 🖼 icon in the format bar, swipe up to view more images, then click on a photo or video to include it to your email.

- To insert a document, tap the 📄 icon above the keyboard and search for the document you want to attach.
  - ✓ In the Files app, click on either **Recents** or **Browse** at the end of your screen, then click on a location, file, or folder to open it.

- Click on the document to insert it to your email.

- A faster way to insert a document is to drag the file you want to attach and drop it on the email screen.

Scan a Document to Your Email

To scan a document into an email,

- Tap the ⬚ icon above the keyboard, then position your iPhone camera to cover the document. Your iPhone automatically captures once the document page appears on your screen.

- To manually capture the press, press any of the volume buttons or tap ◯. Tap the ⚡ enable or disable flash.

- Scan all the pages of the document and tap **Save** to finish.

- To edit the saved scan, click on it, then tap ⬚ to crop the image, ⬤ to apply a filter, ⬚ to rotate the image or 🗑 to delete.

To take a video or photo and insert into an email,

- Tap the 📷 icon above the keyboard and then take a new video or photo.

- Tap **Use Video** or **Use Photo** to insert the video or photo into your email. Tap **Retake** to reshoot your video or photo.

Markup an Attachment

You can use the Markup feature to draw or write on a PDF, video, or photo attachment.

- Open the Mail app and click on an email to open it.

- Click on the attachment to open it, then tap 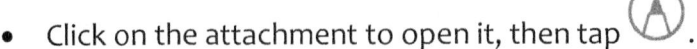.

- Use the drawing tools to draw or write on the document, then tap **Done** to save.

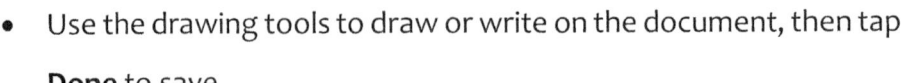

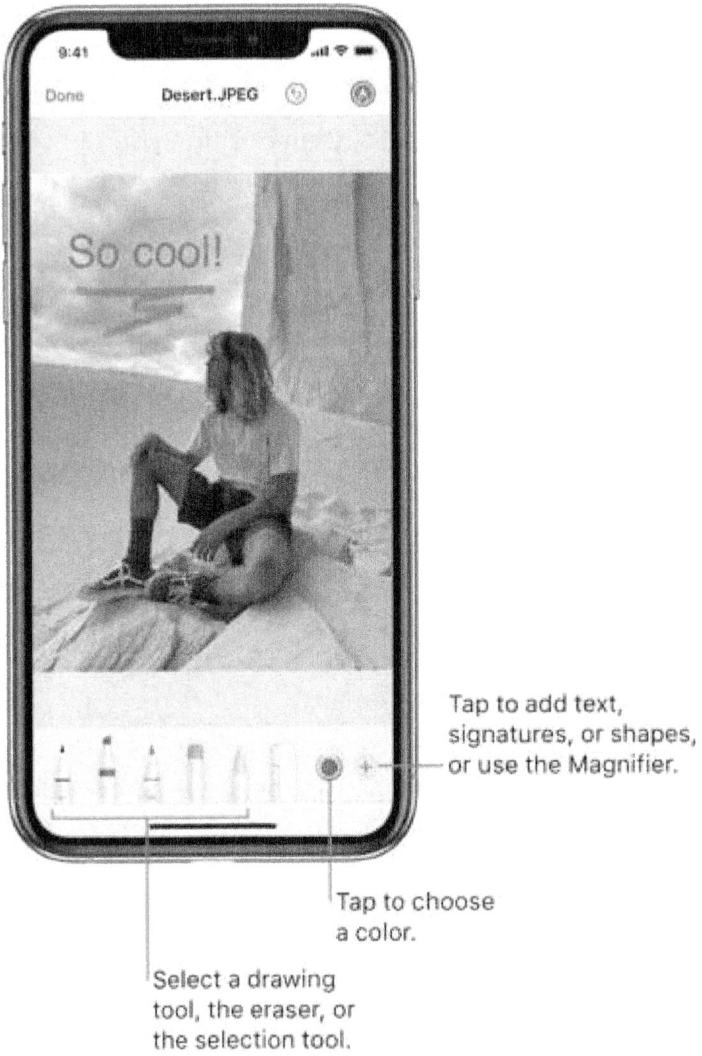

Tap to add text, signatures, or shapes, or use the Magnifier.

Tap to choose a color.

Select a drawing tool, the eraser, or the selection tool.

Draw in Your Email

You can draw right in an email before you send the email.

- Begin typing your response in the email, then tap the ⟨ icon above the keyboard.

- Tap the Ⓐ icon in the format bar.

- Choose the color or a drawing tool, then draw or write with your finger.

- Tap **Done** when you finish editing and then click on **Insert Drawing.**

- To continue working on a drawing, click on the drawing and then tap Ⓐ.

Automatically Copy Yourself

You can set the Mail app to always put you in BCC for every mail that you send.

- Go to Settings on your phone and tap **Mail.**

- Then toggle on **Always BCC Myself.**

Add Additional Mail Accounts

To set up other mail accounts on your phone,

- Go to Settings on your phone and tap **Mail.**

- Click on **Add Account,** then tap **Other.**

- Click on **Add Mail Account,** input your email address and password, then click on **Next.**

- Input the names of the mail servers for the account and other requested information on your screen, then tap **Save.**

Customize Your Email Signature

The signature is the sign off that appears at the end of all the emails you send.

- Go to Settings on your phone and tap **Mail.**
- Click on **Signature,** then click on the text field at the top corner of your screen and edit your signature.
- If you have multiple email account, click on **Per Account** to create a different signature for the different email accounts.

Mark Addresses Outside Certain Domains

You can customize the Mail app to give you a red alert whenever you address an email to an email address that is not in your organization's domain. Any email address that is not in your organization's domain will show in red when you are addressing an email.

- Go to Settings on your phone and tap **Mail.**
- Click on **Mark Addresses,** and input the domains that are in your organization. You can enter more than one domains separated by commas.

Show a Longer Preview

By default, the Mail app displays two lines of text for each email in your mailbox lists. You can configure the app to show more lines of text without opening the received email.

- Go to Settings on your phone and tap **Mail.**
- Tap **Preview,** then choose your preferred option, up to five lines. To show the whole conversation,

- Go to Settings on your phone and tap **Mail.**

- Then toggle on **Organize by Thread.**

Show the CC and To Labels

To show the CC and To labels in your inbox,

- Go to Settings on your phone and tap **Mail.**

- Then toggle on **Show To/Cc Labels.**

Add a Contact from Received Email

- Open the email from the contact you want to save.

- Click on the person's email address or name, then tap **Add to Existing Contacts,** or **Create New Contact.**

Save a Draft

- Open the mail app, begin writing an email, then tap Cancel, and click on **Save Draft.**

- To resume working on the saved draft email, tap and hold the icon and choose a draft.

Flag an Email

Flagging an email makes it easy for you to find it later, as the email will appear in your inbox and Flagged mailbox. To view your flagged emails,

- Open the Mail app, click on **Mailboxes** at the upper left side of your screen. Tap **Edit** and then choose **Flagged.**

To flag an email,

- Open the email, click , then click **Flag.**

- Tap a colored dot to select a color for the flag.

- To remove or change a flag, open the email, click 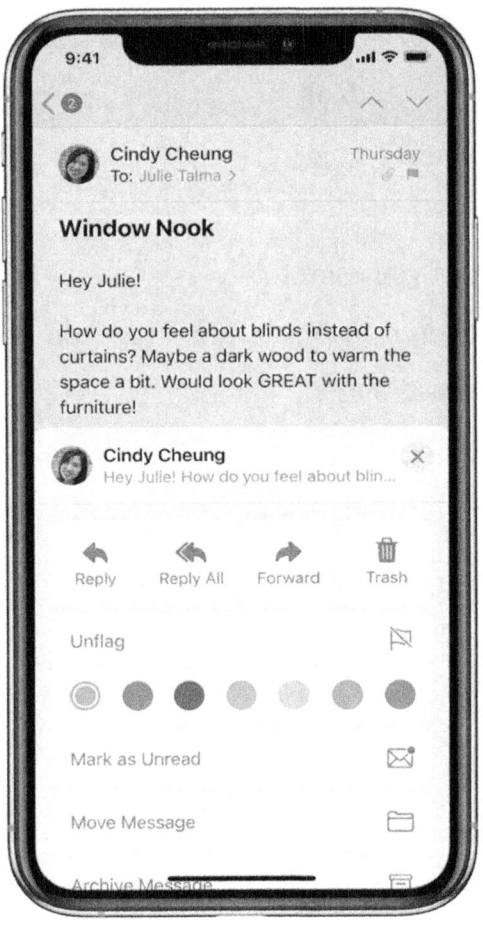, and choose a different color or tap ⚐to unflag.

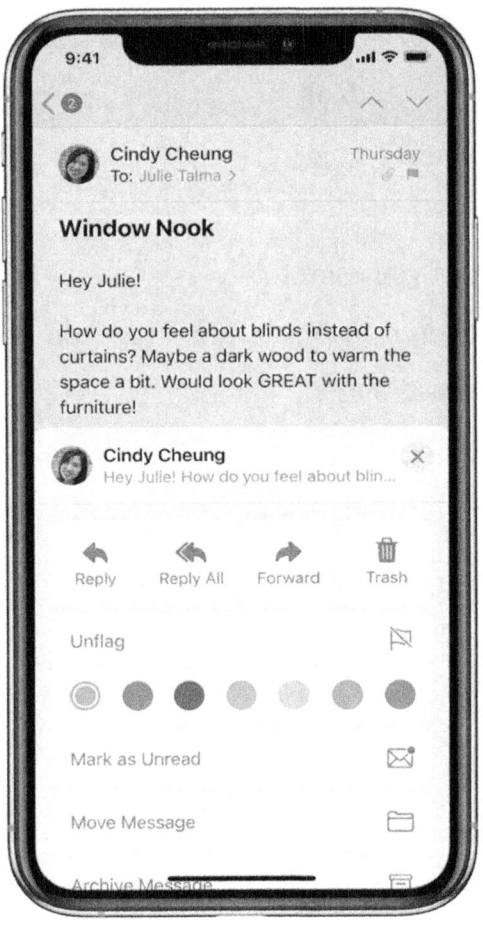

Receive Notification of Replies to an Email

You can create a mail notification to be notified when someone replies to your email or thread:

- To create the notification while reading an email, tap ↩and then click on **Notify Me.**

- To set the notification when writing an email, click on the Subject field and tap 🔔, then click on **Notify Me.**

To allow notifications for the Mail app,

- Go to Settings on your phone and tap **Notification.**
- Tap **Mail,** then turn on **Allow Notifications.**

Mute Email Notifications

You can mute notifications of messages received in busy email threads.

- Open an email in the Mail app, tap ↰ and then click on **Mute.**

To further customize what should be done with muted emails,

- Go to Settings on your phone and tap **Mail.**
- Tap **Muted Thread Action,** and choose your preference.

Block Email from Specified Senders

To block a sender in the Mail app,

- Open an email from them and tap their email address, then click on **Block This Contact.**

Filter Emails

Use the filter to show only emails that meet your preset criteria. For example, if you filter using **Unread,** you will only see unread emails.

- Tap the ⊜ icon in the bottom-left part of a mailbox list.
- Click on **Filtered By,** and choose the criteria you want.

- Tap the ⬇ icon in the bottom-left part to hide emails that do not match your filter selection. Click on the icon again to turn off the filter.

Manage Junk Mail

To move a message to your Junk folder,

- Open the email, tap ↰ and then click on **Move to Junk.**
- If you moved an email in error, instantly swipe left with three fingers to undo the action.

Organize Your Mail with Mailboxes

The Mailboxes list will show you all your mailboxes. You can also delete a mailbox, create a new one, rename an existing one, or reorder your mailboxes.

- Open the Mail app and tap **Mailboxes** at the top left corner.
- Click on **Edit,** and tick the checkboxes beside the mailbox you want to view.
- Scroll to the end of the list and tap **New Mailbox** if you want to add a mailbox. Input a name for the mailbox, choose a location, and then tap **Save.**
- To reorder the mailboxes, press firmly on the ☰ icon beside a mailbox until it lifts, then pull it to any position.

Mark or Move Multiple Emails

- Open the Mail app and tap **Edit.**

- Tap the checkboxes of all the emails you want to mark or move. Swipe down through the checkboxes to quickly select the emails.

- Then choose an action for the selected emails. Swipe left with your three fingers to undo the action.

Show Draft Emails

To view your draft emails from all your mailboxes,

- Open the Mail app and tap **Mailboxes** at the top left corner.

- Click on **Edit,** tap **Add Mailbox,** then toggle on the **All Drafts** mailbox.

Search for an Email

There are different criteria to use in searching for emails in the Mail app

To search for text,

- Swipe down from the center of the mailbox list to show the search field.

- Click on the search field and enter a text or a timeframe like the January meeting.

- Choose to search all the mailboxes or just the current mailbox.

- Click on an email in the displayed list to open it.

You can also search using email attributes:

- To see your flagged emails, type **Flag** in the search field and then click on **Flagged Messages** below **Other.**

- To see emails with attachment, type **Attachment** in the search area, then click on **Messages with Attachments.**

- To find your unread mails, type **Unread,** and then click on **Unread Messages.**
- To find the emails from people in your VIP list, type **VIP,** and then click on **Messages from VIPs.**

Delete Emails

- To delete an email while viewing it, scroll to the end of the page and tap .
- To delete an email while viewing the email list, swipe left on the email and then tap **Trash.** To delete in one movement, swipe the email all the way to the left edge of your screen.
- To delete more than one email at once while viewing the email list, tap **Edit,** choose the emails you wish to delete, then click on **Trash.**
- If you deleted an email in error, instantly swipe left with three fingers to undo the action.

To enable or disable the confirmation of deletion,

- Go to Settings on your phone and tap **Mail.**
- Then disable or enable **Ask Before Deleting.**

Recovered Deleted Emails

- Open the Mail app and click on the **Trash** mailbox.
- Click on an email to open it, tap then move the message to a different mailbox.
- Instantly swipe left with three fingers to undo the action.

To view all the deleted messages across all your account,

- Click on **Mailboxes** at the top left corner of your screen, tap **Edit,** then choose **All Trash.**

Archive Emails

you can archive unwanted emails rather than deleting them. These emails will be stored in the Archive mailbox. To set up Archiving,

- Go to Settings ⚙ on your phone and tap **Mail.**
- Tap **Accounts** and click your email account.
- Click on **Mail** below **Advanced,** then click on **Advanced.**
- Then change the destination mailbox for discarded emails to **Archive Mailbox.**

When you want to delete an email and have the archive option on, press firmly on 🗃 and then click on **Trash Message.**

Set Duration for Deleted Emails

To set a duration for keeping the deleted emails in the Trash mailbox,

- Go to Settings on your phone and tap **Mail.**
- Tap **Accounts** and click your email account.
- Click on **Mail** below **Advanced,** then click on **Advanced.**
- Tap **Remove** and choose a time interval.

Preview, Open or Save an Attachment

If an email contains a document, video, or photo attachment, follow the steps below to preview, open, and save the attachment:

- Press down on the attachment to preview it and view a list of actions that you can perform.

- To save a video or photo, press firmly on the attachment and tap **Add to Photos.**

- To open the attachment with a different app, press firmly on the attachment until you see the menu, then tap ⬆️ and choose the new app for opening the attachment.

Print an Email or Attachment

To print an email,

- Open the email, tap ↩️ and then click on **Print.**

- To print an attachment, click on the attachment to open it, tap ⬆️ and click on **Print.**

Chapter 19: File App

You can use the Files app on your iPhone to access a document stored on external servers or devices like the file servers, SD cards, USB drives, and other storage providers like Dropbox and Box, after you connect them to your phone.

Connect an SD Card or USB Drive to your Phone

- Insert a Lightning to SD Card Camera Reader, Lightning to USB 3 Camera Adapter, or Lightning to USB Camera Adapter into the charging port on your iPhone.

- Then connect your USB drive to the camera adapter using the USB cable that came with the USB drive or insert an SD memory card into the card reader.

- To see the contents stored on the device, open the Files app, tap **Browse** at the bottom, then scroll to **Locations** and click on the USB drive or SD card name. If you don't see **Locations,** scroll to the end of your screen and tap **Browse** again.

- Remove the device from the connector to disconnect it from your phone.

Connect to a File Server or a Computer

To connect to a network server,

- Open the Files app and tap ••• at the top of the **Browse** screen.

- Select **Connect to Server,** enter a network address or a local hostname and then tap **Connect.**

- Once connected, you will see the file server or computer in the **Recent Servers** list on the **"Connect to Server"** screen. Click on a name to connect to a recent server.

- Then choose how you wish to connect, either as a Guest or as a Registered User. Enter your user name and password if connecting as a registered user.

- Tap **Next** and choose a shared folder or the server volume on the next screen.

- Tap the icon next to the server in the Browse screen to disconnect from the file server.

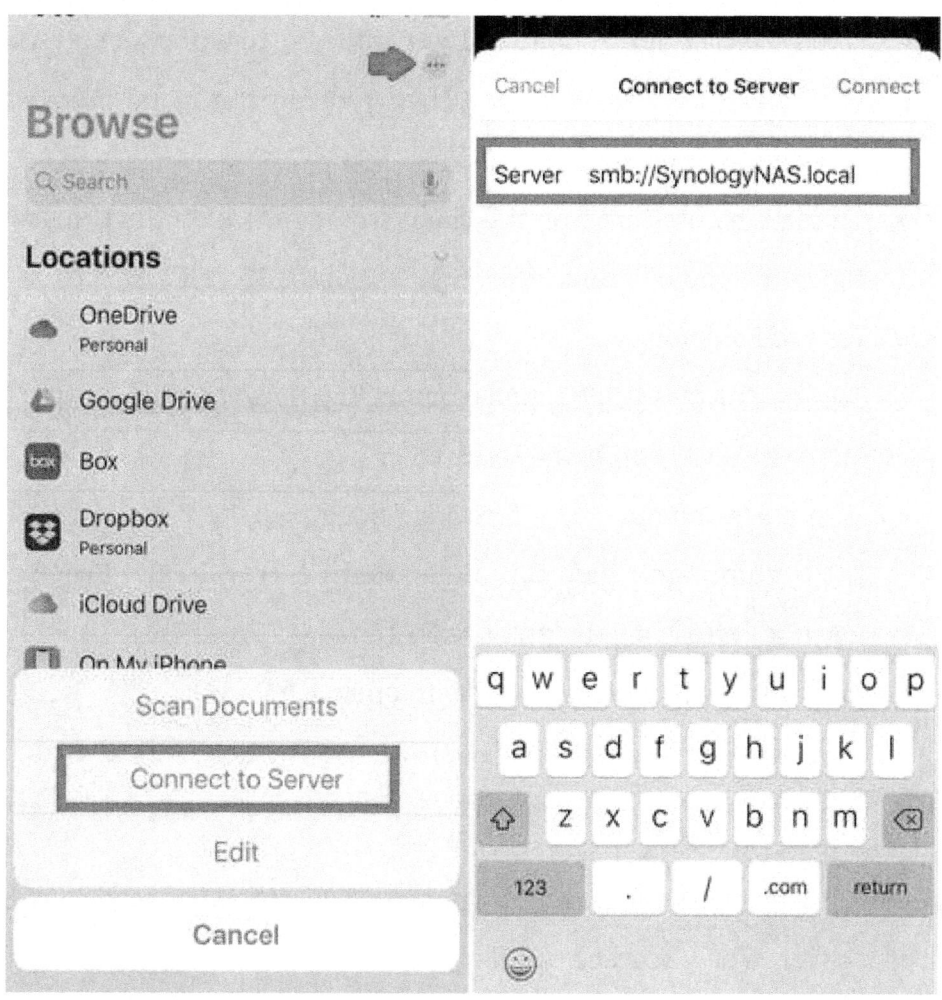

Add a Cloud Storage Service

Your iPhone only comes with free 5GB of cloud storage. If you experience space constraints, you may need to download cloud storage apps like Dropbox, OneDrive, Google Drive, etc. Download any of these apps from the Apple Store, launch the app, and follow the instructions on your screen to complete. Once done, follow the steps below to add it to the Files app:

- Open the Files app and tap **Browse** at the bottom of your screen.

- Click on **More Locations** and then turn on the cloud storage service you downloaded.

- To see what is stored on the cloud storage, click on the **Browse** tab at the end of your screen, then select the storage service.

View Files and Folders

- To view the files you opened recently, tap **Recents** at the bottom left of the Files app home screen.

- To browse and open your files and folders, tap the **Browse** tab at the bottom right, then click on an item to open it. Tap **Browse** again to refresh if you don't see an item.

- Click on a folder, location, or file to open it.

- To search for a specific folder or file, tap the Search field at the top of your screen and enter the folder name, document type, or file name. Click on a result to open it or tap ⊗ in the search field to start a new search.

Switch Between Icon or List View

To change the way the folders are displayed,

- Open the File app and click on an existing folder or location like **iCloud Drive.**

- Drag down from the center of your screen and then tap the icon to switch between **List** view or **Icon** view.

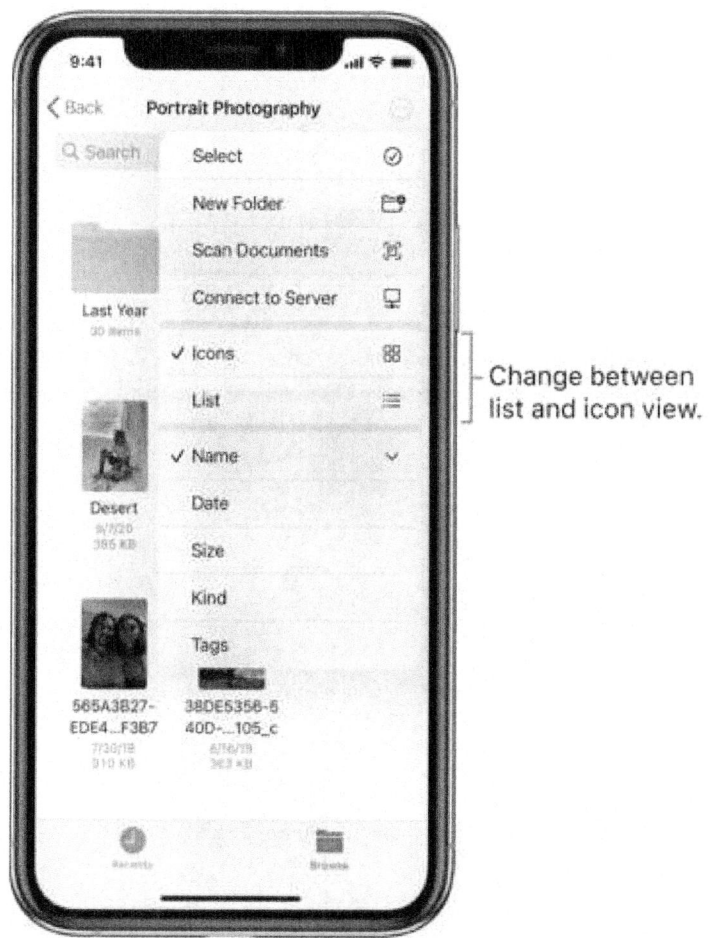

Change between list and icon view.

Change How Folders and Files are Sorted

Follow the steps below to change the way your folders and files are sorted:

- Open the File app and click on an existing folder or location like **iCloud Drive.**

- Then drag down from the center of your screen.

- Click on **Sorted By,** and then choose an option from the list on your screen.

Rearrange the Browse Screen

- Open the Files app and tap **Browse** at the bottom of your screen.

- Tap ⦁⦁⦁ and then tap **Edit.**

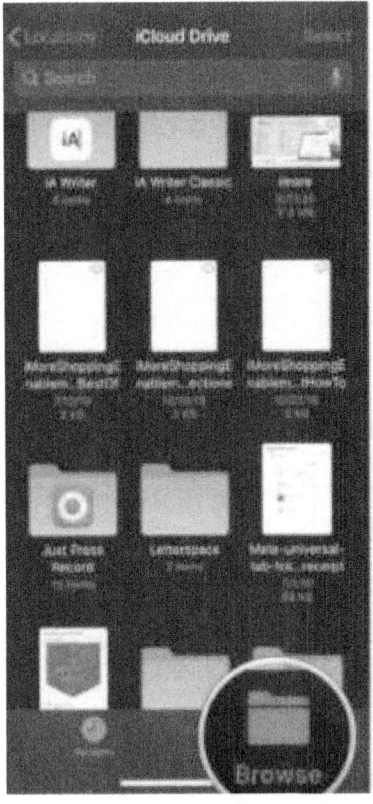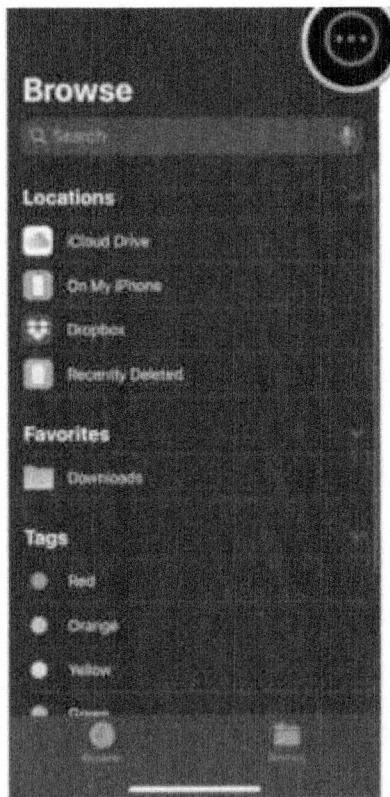

- Under **Location,** turn any location on or off to hide or unhide the location.

- Tap the ⊖ icon next to a tag to delete the tag and remove it from all items.

- Tap the ⊖ icon next to a folder to remove the folder from the Favorites list.

- To reorder the folders or items, tap and hold the ≡ icon beside an item and drag it to a different position.

- Tap **Done** to save your changes.

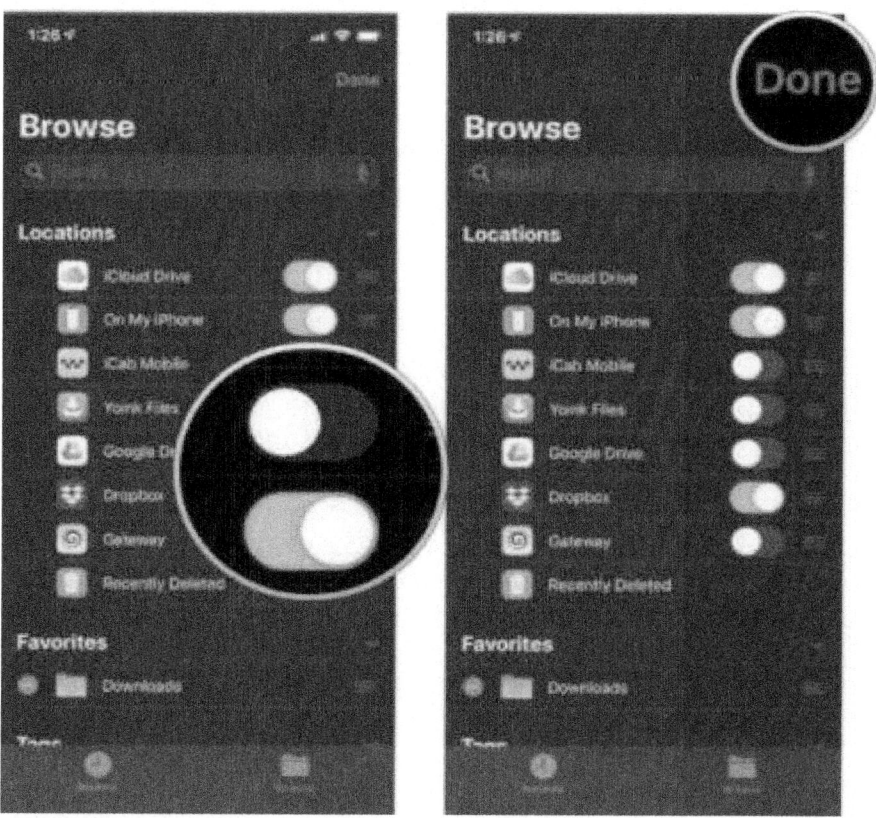

Create a Folder

Folders help you to organize images, documents, and other files on your phone.

- Open the File app and click on an existing folder or location like **iCloud Drive.**

- Drag down from the center of your screen and tap the ••• icon and then choose **New Folder.**

- You will be unable to create a folder in the location you choose if you do not see the **New Folder** option.

Edit a Folder or File

See below how to compress, rename, and make other changes to a folder or file:

- Tap and hold the folder or file, then choose an option on your screen: **Duplicate, Delete, Copy, Rename, Move,** or **Compress.**

- To modify more than one folder simultaneously, tap Select at the top of your screen, make your selections, and then click on an option at the bottom of your screen.

Tag a Folder or File

Tags make it easy for you to search and find the folder in the future:

- Tap and hold a folder or file, click on **Tags,** and select one or more tags.

- Then tap **Done.**

To find your tagged items,

- Tap the **Browse** tab at the bottom of your screen, and then click on an item below **Tags.**

- Click on a tag to remove the tag.

Mark a Folder as Favorite

- Tap and hold the folder and then click on **Favorite.**

- To find your favorite folders, tap the **Browse** tab, and click on the folder in the **Favorite** section.

Send Files from your Phone

To share a file on your iPhone with others,

- Open the Files app and go to the file you wish to share.

- Tap and hold the file, then click on **Share.**

- To send a smaller version of the file, click on **Compress,** then hold the file's compressed version and click on **Share.**

- Choose your option for sending and then click on **Send.**

Scan a Document

If you want to send a document that is not yet digitized, you can scan the document with the Files app first before sending it.

- Open the Files app and tap **Browse** at the bottom of your screen.

- Tap   and then tap **Scan Documents.**

Set up iCloud Drive on iPhone

You can use the Files app to store folders and files in the iCloud Drive. You can then access the files from any device that uses the same Apple ID. Any change made on one device will appear on all the other devices. First, you will need to turn on iCloud Drive. See the steps below:

- Go to Settings on your phone and tap your name.

- Click on **iCloud,** then toggle on **iCloud Drive.**

- Toggle on all the apps that you want to use with iCloud Drive.

Browse iCloud Drive

From the Files app, you can see all that you stored on iCloud Drive. You can also invite people to view or change content on your iCloud Drive. You can choose the people who can access a shared folder and make changes to the folder. Only the invited people can access your shared files.

- Open the Files app and click the **Browse** tab at the bottom.
- Tap **iCloud Drive** and click on a folder to open it.
- To share a file or folder, touch and hold the file, tap **Share** and then click on **Add People.**
- Now do one of the following:
  - ➢ If you want your invitees to view and edit the shared document, click on **Share Options,** choose **Only People You Invite,** then select **Can Make Changes.** Once done, choose a method for sending the link to the invitees.
  - ➢ If you want the invitees to only view the content, click on **Share Options,** choose **Only People You Invite,** then select **View Only.**
  - ➢ If you want anyone with the link to view and modify the shared document, click on **Share Options,** choose **Anyone with the Link,** then select **Can Make Changes.** Select **View Only** if you want this category of people to only view the content without making any changes.
- Select the sharing method and tap **Send.**

138

Invite More People to Share a File or Folder

If you shared a file with the access set to **"Only People You Invite,"** follow the steps below to share the file with more people:

- Touch and hold the file, tap **Share** and then click on **Show People.**
- Click on **Add People** and choose a method for sending the invite.
- Input all the requested information and then send the invitation.

Share a File or Folder Using a Link

If you shared a file with the access set to **"Anyone with the Link,"** people with the link will be able to share the file with others. To add more people:

- Touch and hold the file, tap **Share** and then click on **Show People.**
- Click on **Send Link** and choose a method for sending the invite.
- Input all the requested information and then send the invitation.

Change Permission Settings and Access

As the shared folder or file owner, any changes you make to a shared link will affect other users. To change access and permission settings,

- Touch and hold the file, tap **Share** and then click on **Show People.**
- Click on **Share Options,** then choose from the options on your screen:

- ➢ If you change the access settings from **Anyone with the Link** to **Only People You Invite,** the initial link will be revoked for anyone, and a new link sent to the invited participants.
- ➢ If you change the permission settings, invitees with the file open will receive an alert, and the new settings will take effect once they dismiss the alert.

To change the permission settings for one person without affecting other users,

- ➢ Press down on the file or folder, tap **Share** and then click on **Show People.**
- ➢ Click on the person's name and choose an option.

Stop Sharing a File or Folder

- ➢ Press down on the file or folder, tap **Share** and then click on **Show People.**
- ➢ Then click on **Stop Sharing.**
- ➢ This setting will remove the document from every invitees' iCloud Drive. The shared link will also stop working.

Chapter 20: Shortcut App

A shortcut gives you a quick way to do things with your apps by tapping a button or asking Siri. Shortcuts help to automate several functions, like generating expense reports, moving text from one app to another, and more. Siri checks your app usage, your email, messaging, and browser history to suggest simple and useful shortcuts that you can tap to run. After you create a shortcut, you can summon Siri and ask him to run one of the shortcuts.

The Shortcut app on your phone allows you to add custom or ready-made shortcuts to your device. The app also allows you to combine several steps across different apps to create powerful task automation.

For instance, you can create a "Surf Time" shortcut that can give you ETA to the beach, get you the surf report, and launch your surf music playlist, all these by tapping the Surf Time shortcut.

What is an Action?

Actions are what make up a shortcut. Each shortcut you create has several actions, and each action is a single step that performs a specific function. For instance, if you have a shortcut that shares an animated GIF, the shortcut may contain three different actions, one for grabbing the latest photos on your device, the second action uses the photos to build an animated GIF, while the third action sends the GIF to your recipients.

Create a New Shortcut

- Open the **Shortcut** app on your phone and tap **My Shortcuts** at the bottom.

- Tap ╋ at the top right side of your screen to see an empty, untitled shortcut in the shortcut editor.

- Tap **Add Action** and a list of action categories will appear.

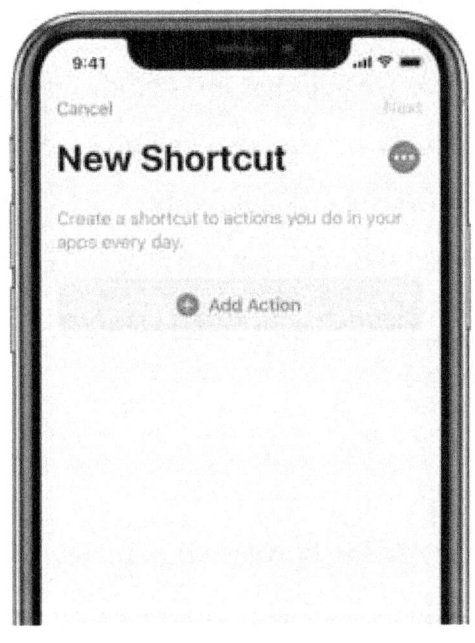

- Select an action to add it to your shortcut. Or, press firmly on an action in the list, then drag it and drop in the shortcut editor.

- To add more actions, tap ➕ and select the new action. Tapping the icon will display the action category you choose previously. Tap ✖ to return to a list of all the action categories.

- Add all the actions you want, tap Next, choose a name for the shortcuts, and then tap **Done.**

- Return to the home screen to see all your shortcuts.

- To open a shortcut, tap the ⬤ icon on the shortcut, then tap ▶ to play. Tap ◼ to stop the shortcut.

- To give the shortcut a new name, tap ⬤ , tap the shortcut name, set up the new name, then tap **Done** to save your changes.

Tip: a quick way to create a shortcut: touch and hold the shortcuts app icon on your phone's home screen then tap **Create Shortcut.**

Undo or Redo Steps while Composing Your Shortcuts

While creating your shortcuts, you can undo or redo steps:

- Tap the ↻ or ↺ icons in the shortcut editor to redo or undo your steps.

- Tap ✕ on an action to delete it from the shortcut editor.

View Information about an Action

You can view details of every action you add to your shortcut, sort the list of available actions, and even create favorite actions. Some apps may need you to grant permission to the shortcut before you can use an application shortcut. To do this, simply tap **Allow Access** in the action screen.

To view details about an action

- Open the **Shortcut** app and tap **My Shortcuts** .

- Tap the icon on a shortcut to open the shortcut editor.

- Tap to bring up a list of action categories.

- Click on an action category, then tap (i) for a specific action to view a brief description of the action.

Note: if you want to view details for an action that you created already, click on the action's icon or name on the app's home screen.

View All Actions in a Category

See below how to view the actions that are in one category:

- Open the **Shortcut** app and tap **My Shortcuts** .

- Tap the icon on a shortcut to open the shortcut editor.

- Tap to bring up a list of action categories.

- Select a category name to view all the actions for that category.

View Actions Suggested by Siri

Siri suggests actions for us based on your use of your device. To view these Siri suggested actions,

- Open the **Shortcut** app and tap **My Shortcuts** .

- Tap the icon on a shortcut to open the shortcut editor.

- Tap $\mathcal{Q}$ to bring up a list of action categories.

- Scroll down to view the Siri suggestions.

- Tap the (i) icon to view an action's description.

Favorite an Action

- Open the **Shortcut** app and tap **My Shortcuts** ▪▪.

- Tap the ••• icon on a shortcut to open the shortcut editor.

- Tap the icon of the action you wish to mark as favorite, then tap

  ★ . The action will be added to your Favorite list.

To view your favorite actions,

- Tap the $\mathcal{Q}$ icon in the shortcut editor, and then click on **Favorites.**

Duplicate a Shortcut

To create more than one version of a shortcut,

- Open the Shortcut app and tap **My Shortcuts** ▪▪.

- Click on **Select,** choose all the actions you want to duplicate, then tap **Duplicate** at the bottom of your screen.

- Tap **Done** to save.

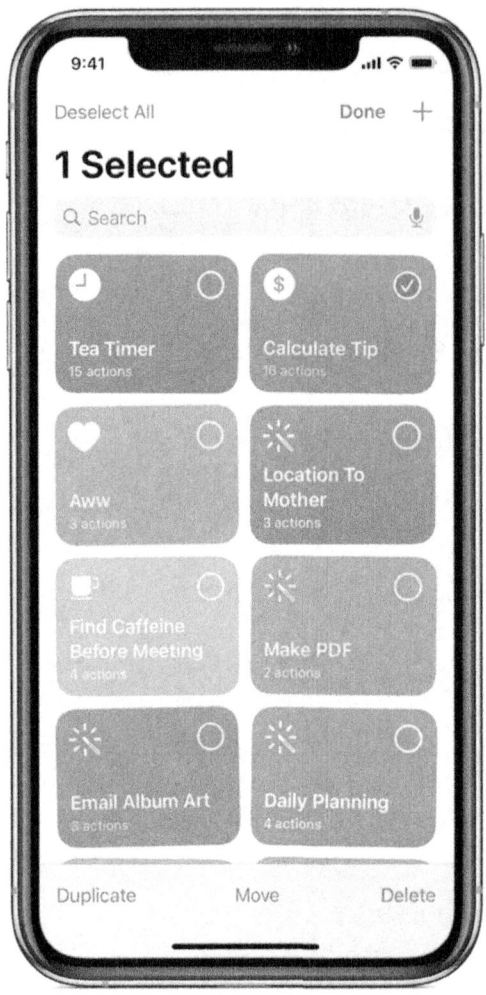

There is a quick way to duplicate one shortcut.

- Touch and hold the Shortcut in the home screen of the shortcut app, then tap **Duplicate.**

Delete a Shortcut

- Open the Shortcut app and tap **My Shortcuts** .
- Click on **Select,** choose all the actions you want to delete, then tap **Delete** at the bottom of your screen.

- Then tap **Delete (number) Shortcuts.**

There is a quick way to delete one shortcut.

- Touch and hold the Shortcut in the home screen of the shortcut app, then tap **Delete.**

Chapter 21: Browse and Play Music

To play music on your phone,

- Open the Music app and tap **Library.**

- Click on a category like **Songs** or **Albums;** click on **Downloaded** to see only the music you have on your iPhone.

- Browse through the music or use the search field to look for particular music – swipe down the page, then enter your search term in the search field.

- Tap a song, then tap **Play.** Click **Shuffle** to shuffle the playlist or album. Or, press firmly on the album art and tap **Play.**

You can also change the list of categories visible on your screen:

- Tap **Edit,** then choose the different categories you want to add to your Music app.

- Click on an existing category to remove it from your app.

Sort Your Music

- Open the Music app and tap **Library.**

- Tap **Music Videos, Albums, TV& Movies, Songs,** or **Playlists.**

- Tap **Sort,** then choose your preferred sorting method.

Play Music Shared on a Nearby Computer

If you have a nearby computer on your network that shares music using Home Sharing, follow the steps below to stream its music to your phone.

- Go to **Settings** on your phone and tap **Music.**

- Scroll to **Home Sharing,** tap **Sign in,** then enter your Apple ID to sign in.

- Now launch the Music app 🎵, tap **Library.**
- Click on **Home Sharing,** then select a shared library.

Remove Apple Music Songs

To remove Apple Music songs stored on your phone, follow the steps below. Note that the music will remain in iCloud. This will not also affect the music you synced or purchased.

- Go to **Settings** on your phone.
- Tap **Music,** then toggle off **Sync Library**

Stream Music to Airplay Enabled or Bluetooth devices

- Click on the player to launch **Now Playing.**
- Then tap the 📡 icon and choose the device you want to use to stream music.

Queue Up Your Music

The queue in the Music app has a list of upcoming songs. You can also add videos & songs to the queue as well as see what you played recently.

- Click the player to launch **Now Playing.**
- Tap ☰ icon and swipe down to view your played history.
- Tap **Clear** to remove the playing history.
- Click on a song on the list to play it and all the songs after it.
- Drag the ☰ icon beside a song to reorder the list.
- Tap the ☰ icon again to hide the queue.

The Autoplay feature automatically adds music to the end of your queue using what you last played. Tap the ∞ icon to turn off Autoplay. When you turn off Autoplay on one device, the feature will also be disabled across other devices that use the same Apple ID.

Add Music and Videos to the Queue

To manually add music and videos to the queue

- Open the player to launch **Now Playing,** then press firmly on a video, song, playlist, or album.

- Tap **Play next** to add the music immediately after the currently playing item.

- Tap **Play Last** to add it to the end of the queue.

Subscribe to Apple Music

Apple Music offers users a full Apple Music catalog, on-demand radio stations, and expert recommendations. When you open the Music app for the first time, you will receive a prompt to subscribe to Apple Music. You can skip and subscribe later. To subscribe later,

- Go to **Settings** on your phone.

- Tap **Music,** then click on **Start Free Trial.**

- To hide or show subscription features, toggle on or off **Show Apple Music.**

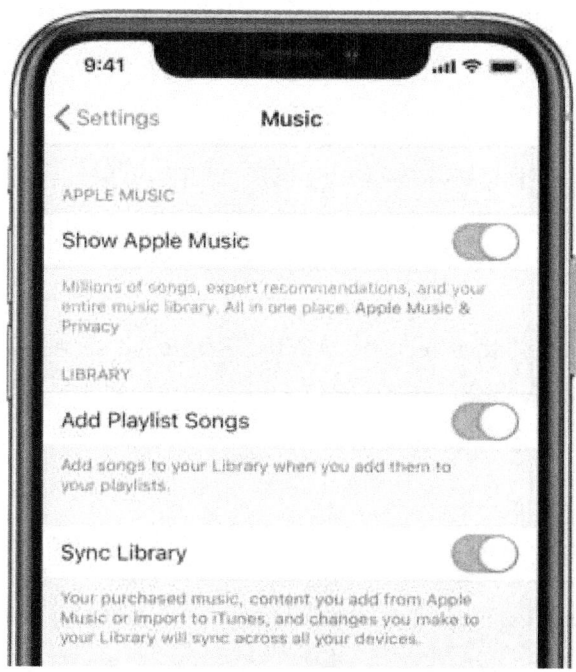

Choose Cellular Data Options for Music

To set up your cellular data option when using the Music app,

- Go to **Settings** on your phone.
- Tap **Music,** then click on **Cellular.** Now choose from the option on your screen as you prefer.

Modify Your Subscription

To cancel or change your subscription plan

- Click on **Listen Now,** then click on your profile picture or tap
- Tap **Manage Subscription** to cancel or change.

Add Music from Apple Music to your Library

There are several ways to do this.

1. Click on the player to launch **Now Playing, t**ap ● ● ● , then click on **Add to Library.**

2. Open the Apple Music app, scroll to the music, video, album, or playlist you want to add and press firmly on it, then select **Add to Library.**

3. Open the content of a playlist or an album in the Apple Music app, then tap ╈ to add a single song or tap **Add** to add a playlist or album.

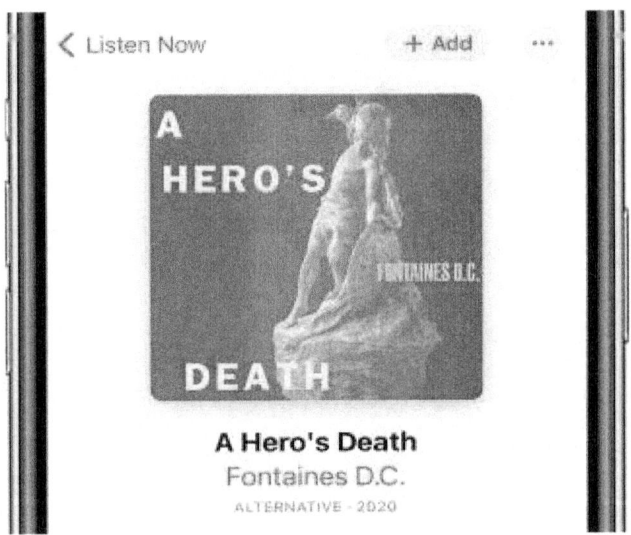

To delete content from your library,

- Press firmly on the music or video and then tap **Delete from Library.**

Every music you add to your phone will also be added to other devices using the same Apple ID and have the iCloud Music Library enabled.

Add Music to a Playlist

- Open the Apple Music app.

- Scroll to the music, video, album, or playlist you want to add and press firmly on it, then select **Add to a Playlist.** Then choose the playlist you want.

Download Music from Apple Music to your Phone

- Open the Apple Music app.

- Open the content that you want to download, then tap 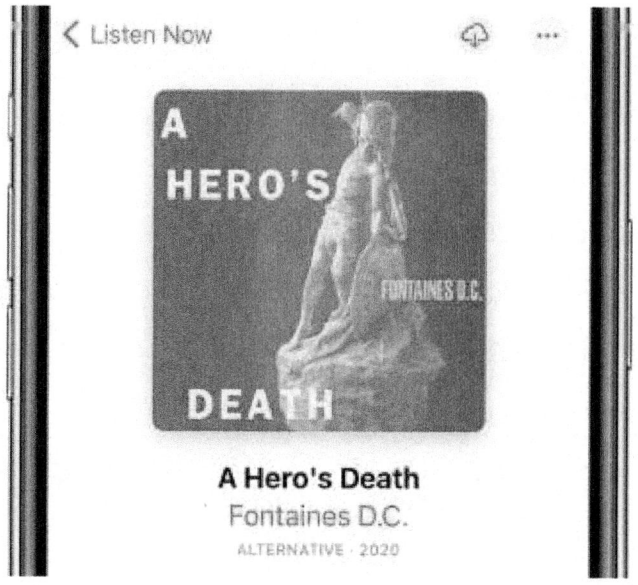 at the top of your screen.

Before you can download music from Apple Music to your phone, you need to turn on **Sync Library.** To do this,

- Go to **Settings** on your phone.

- Tap **Music,** then turn on **Sync Library.**

To turn on automatic download from Apple Music,

- Go to **Settings** on your phone.
- Tap **Music,** then turn on **Automatic Downloads.**
- So whenever you add songs to the Apple Music, they are automatically downloaded to your phone.

To see the download progress,

- Go to the Library tab on the app, click on **Downloaded Music,** and then click **Downloading.**

Manage Storage Space

To automatically remove the music that you haven't played in a while,

- Go to **Settings** on your phone.
- Tap **Music,** then click on **Optimize Storage.**

To delete videos and music stored on your phone,

- Press down on a music video, TV show, playlist, album, movie, or song that you downloaded.
- Tap **Download,** then click on **Remove Downloads.**

To delete all the songs on your phone or to remove songs from a specific artist,

- Go to **Settings** on your phone.
- Tap **Music,** then click on **Downloaded Music.**
- Tap **Edit,** then click the button beside **All Songs** or the artist that owns the music you want to delete.

See Recommended Music

Apple Music studies your music likes and recommends playlists, albums, and songs based on your taste. The Music app Listen Now section helps you find and play contents from your favorite albums, unique mixes, interviews, and playlists based on your taste.

The first time you click on **Listen Now,** you will receive a prompt to inform Apple Music about your preferences, which Apple Music uses to recommend music to you. To select your favorite artists and genres,

- Click on the genres you like, double-click on the ones you love, or press down on the genres you do not want.

- Tap **Next** and repeat the steps in number one for the artists that shows on your screen.

- If an artist isn't listed, click on **Add an Artist** & enter the artist's name.

Play Songs from Apple Music

To play music recommended by Apple Music for you,

- Click on **Listen Now** at the bottom of your screen and tap an album or playlist.

- Tap **Play** or **Shuffle** if you want to shuffle the playlist or album. Or, press firmly on the album art, and tap **Play.**

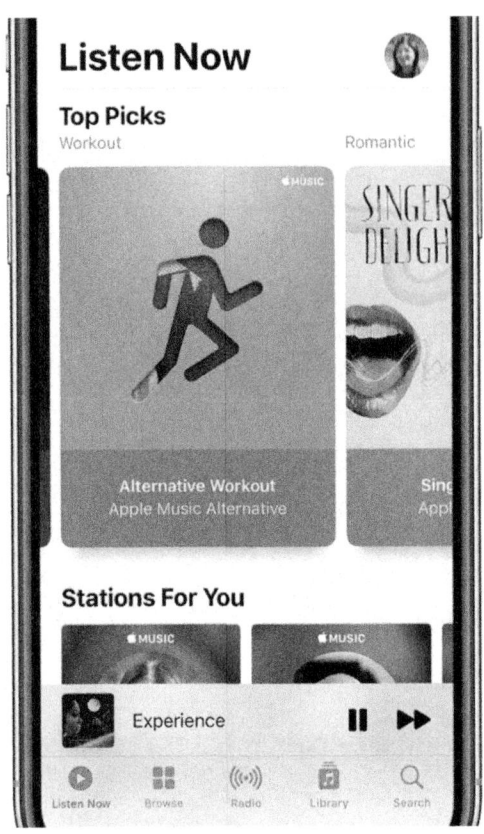

To play songs from an artist's catalog,

- Go to the artist page and tap the ⏵ button close to the top of your screen.
- Apple Music will then play songs from the artist's complete catalog.

Let Apple Music know what you love

Letting Apple Music know what you love and don't love will improve the music recommendations you receive in the future. You can do this in two ways,

- Press down on a playlist, song, or album and then click on **Suggest Less Like This** to dislike a song, or tap **Love** to have more of such songs.

- Open the Now Playing screen, tap ● ● ●, then click on **Suggest Less Like This** to dislike a song, or tap **Love** to have more of such songs.

Rate Music in Your Library

- Go to **Settings** on your phone.
- Tap **Music,** then turn on **Show Star Ratings.**
- Open the Music app, press down on a song in the library, click on **Rate Song,** then choose your rating.

Note that you will only see this option if you already have star ratings from a synced library on your phone.

Tell Music to Ignore Your Listening Habits

You can prevent Apple Music from using your listening habits to influence your Listen Now recommendations.

- Go to **Settings** on your phone.
- Tap **Music,** then turn off **Use Listening History.**

Listen to Apple Music Radio

- Open the Music app and click on the **Radio** tab at the bottom of your screen.
- Then click on one of the Apple Music radio stations to play.

Note that you will be unable to skip or rewind songs.

Listen to Your Favorite Music Genre

- Open the Music app and click on the **Radio** tab at the bottom of your screen.

- Scroll to **Radio by Genre,** and click on a genre, then tap a featured station.

Create a Station

Apple Music radio allows users to create a radio station based on a particular song or artist. You can then go straight to the radio station whenever you want to listen to songs from the selected artist.

- In the Music app's Radio tab, press down on a song or artist, then click on **Create Station.**

You can also create a station while in the Now Playing screen.

- Tap the ••• button and select **Create Station.**

Create Playlists to Organize Your Music

- In the Library tab of the Apple Music app, click on **Playlists,** then select **New Playlist.**

- Enter a name and description for easy identification.

- To choose a playlist cover art, tap and then choose an image from your photo library or capture an image using the camera app.

- Click on **Add Music,** then choose the music you want in the playlist.

Here is another way you can create a playlist

- On the Now Playing screen or in a track list, tap the ● ● ● button.
- Click on **Add to a Playlist** and then tap **New Playlist.**

You can configure your phone to automatically add songs to your library when you add the songs to a playlist.

- Go to **Settings** ⚙ on your phone.
- Tap **Music,** then turn on **Add Playlist Songs.**

Edit a Playlist you Created

- Click on the playlist, then tap ● ● ● .
- Click on **Edit** and then choose from the following:
  - ✓ To add more songs to your playlist, tap **Add Music,** then select the new songs.
  - ✓ To delete a song, click on ⊖ , then tap **Delete.** Note that deleting songs from your playlist will not delete the song from your library.
  - ✓ To change how the songs are ordered, drag the ☰ icon by the side of a song and move it to a different position.

Delete a Playlist

- Press down on the playlist, then click on **Delete from Library.**
- Or, click on the playlist, tap ● ● ● , then click on **Delete from Library.**

See What Your Friends are Listening to

Apple Music subscribers can follow their friends to see the music the friends are listening to. You can also view the playlists they shared. Your followers can also see the music you are listening to as well as your shared playlists. All this information is available on your profile screen in the Music app.

The first time you open the Music app, you will receive a prompt to create a profile and begin following friends. If you skipped this step at the time, you could follow the steps below to create the profile at any time:

- Click **Listen Now,** and click on your profile picture or tap .
- Then click on **Start Sharing with Friends**.
- Click on **View Profile** at the top part of your screen to view your profile.

Follow your Friends

There are more than one ways to follow people in the Music app:

- You can add friends at the point of creating a profile.

- Click **Listen Now,** & click on your profile picture or tap . Swipe to the end of the screen and tap **Follow More Friends,** then click on **Follow** by the side of the persons you want to follow.
- While on your profile screen, press down on a profile picture and tap **Follow.**
- In the profile screen, click on **Search,** type in a name, select the name in the results, then tap **Follow.**

- Swipe up on the profile screen to see those who you follow and those who follow you.

Note that your friends need to have created a profile before you can find them using the search option.

Respond to Follow Requests

You can choose the people who follow you or allow everyone to follow you. The Follow Request only comes if you decide to choose the people that can follow you.

- Click **Listen Now,** and click on your profile picture or tap .
- Click on **View Profile,** tap **Edit,** and click on People You Approve if you wish to be followed only by persons you approve.
- Click on **Follow Requests,** then decline or accepts the requests on your screen.

Stop Following and Block Followers

- Press down on the profile picture of the person, then click on **Unfollow.**

To block followers,

- Press down on the profile picture of the person, then click on **Block.**

Share Music with Followers

By default, your followers can see all your playlists, but you can choose the playlists you do not want to share.

- Click **Listen Now,** then click on your profile picture or tap .

- Click on **View Profile,** tap **Edit,** then disable the playlists you do not want to share.

- Drag the ≡ button to reorder the playlists.

To share a playlist with someone that is not following you,

- Press down on a playlist and then click on **Share Playlist.**

Hide Music from your Followers

- Click **Listen Now,** then click on your profile picture or tap 👤 .

- Click on **View Profile,** scroll to **Listening To,** press down on an album or a playlist, then click on **Hide from Profile.**

The playlist that you hide will not show in your profile, neither will your followers see it. You can also stop your followers from seeing the music you listen to.

- Tap **Edit** on the profile screen, then disable **Listening To.**

See what Others are Listening to

- Click **Listen Now,** then choose any of the following:

  ✓ To see what your followers or person you follow is listening to, click on your profile picture or tap 👤 , then click on **View Profile.** Click on someone's profile picture to see the music they are listening to and their shared playlists.

  ✓ To listen to a mix of songs that your friends listen to, scroll to **Made for You,** swipe left, and then click on **Friends Mix.**

✓ To see what your friends are listening to, navigate to **Friends are Listening to,** then click on a song to play it.

Share Your Profile

You can share your profile with others using Messages, email, or any other app of your choice.

- Click **Listen Now,** then click on your profile picture or tap ⊙ .

- Click on **View Profile,** tap ••• , tap **Share,** then choose your sharing option.

Change the way Music Sounds on your Phone

You can customize music sounds on iPhone with volume limit settings, EQ, and Sound Check.

To choose an EQ (equalization) settings,

- Go to the Settings app on your phone and tap **Music.**

- Then tap **EQ.**

To normalize the volume level of audio on your device,

- Go to the Settings app on your phone and tap **Music.**

- Then enable **Sound Check.**

Chapter 22: Contact App

Create a Contact

- Open the Contacts app and tap ➕.

You may also receive suggestions from Siri to save new contacts based on how you use other apps like the invitations you receive in Calendar and email you receive in Mail. You can follow the steps below to turn off **Siri Suggestions for Contacts:**

- Go to the Settings app on your phone and tap **Contact.**
- Tap **Siri & Search,** then disable **Show Siri Suggestions for Contacts.**

Based on your usage of the Contacts app, Siri also offers contact information suggestions when using other apps. You can follow the steps below to turn off this feature:

- Go to the Settings app on your phone and tap **Contact.**
- Tap **Siri & Search,** then disable **Learn from this App.**

Share a Contact

- Open the Contacts app and click on a contact.
- Tap **Share Contact,** then select a method for sending the contact details.
- To find a contact, click on the search field at the top of the contact list, then input the phone number, address, name, or other search terms.

Quickly Reach a Contact

While in the contacts app, you can make a FaceTime call, start a message, or send money with Apple Pay.

- Open the Contacts app and click on a contact.

- Tap an option below the contact's name to contact or send money to the contact.

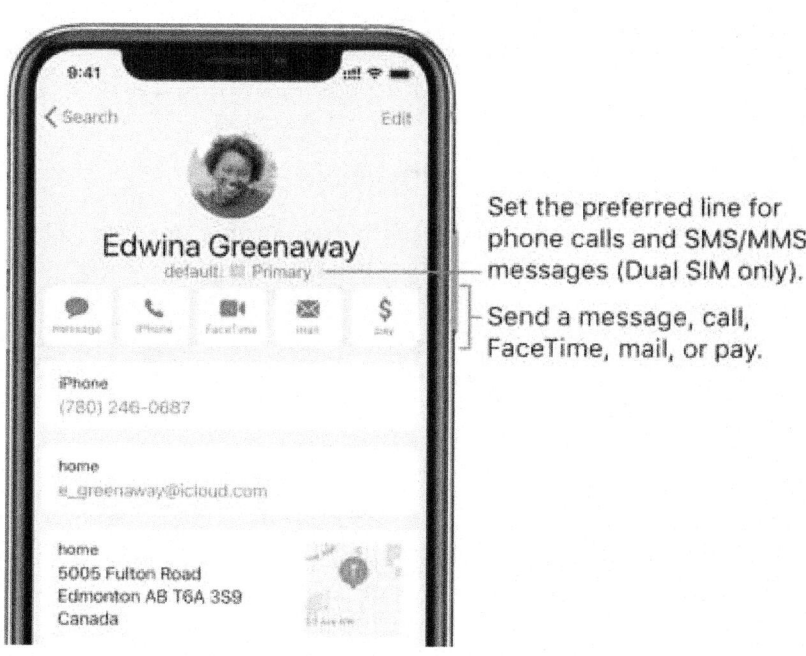

Set the preferred line for phone calls and SMS/MMS messages (Dual SIM only).

Send a message, call, FaceTime, mail, or pay.

Edit Contacts on your iPhone

- Open the Contacts app, click on a contact, then tap **Edit** and do any of the following:

  ✓ To delete a contact, tap **Delete Contact** at the bottom of your screen.

  ✓ To use a photo for a contact, click on **Add Photo,** then add a photo from the photos app or take a new photo.

✓ To change a label for the contact, click on the label, then choose a new label in the list or click on **Custom Label** to create your own label.

✓ Tap the Notes field to add notes for a contact.

✓ To receive texts or calls from a contact while Do Not Disturb is turned on, click on **Ringtone or Text Tone,** then enable **Emergency Bypass.**

✓ To add a social profile, related name, birthday, and more, tap the ⊕ icon beside each item.

✓ To add a phonetic name, prefix, pronunciation, etc., click on **Add Field** and then choose from the list.

✓ To delete contact information, click on the ⊖ icon next to a field.

- Tap **Done** to save your changes.

Choose a Preferred Line for Calls and Messages

For Dual SIM phones, when you text or call a contact, your phone uses the same line you used for your last communication with this contact by default. To choose a preferred line for messages and phone calls,

- Click on a contact, tap **Default** below the contact's name, and then choose a line for reaching that contact.

Complete My Card

My Card contains your contact information like your name, address, and phone number. To add your information to your contact card,

- Open the Contacts app, click on **My Card** at the top of the screen, then tap **Edit.**

- If there is no My Card, tap the ✛ icon and enter your information.

- Then go to the Settings app on your phone, click on **Contacts,** tap **My Info** and then click on your name in the Contacts list.

Create or Edit Your Medical ID

Medical ID contains your health information, which may be important should you have any health emergency. To create or edit,

- Open the Contacts app, click on **My Card** at the top of the screen, then tap **Edit.**

- Move down and select either **Create Medical ID** or **Edit Medical ID.**

Use Your Contacts Accounts on Your Phone.

You can add contacts from your iCloud or Google contacts to the Contacts app on your phone.

To use your iCloud contacts,

- Go to the Settings app on your phone, tap your name, tap **iCloud,** then switch on **Contacts.**

To use your Google contacts,

- Go to the Settings app on your phone, tap **Contacts**, tap **Google.**

- Sign in to your Google account and then switch on **Contacts.**

To add contacts from another account,

- Go to the Settings app, tap **Contacts**, tap **Add Account.**

- Choose the account and sign in to it, then switch on **Contacts.**

Import Contacts

You can import contacts from a SIM card or a vCard. To import from a SIM card,

- Go to the Settings app on your phone, tap **Contacts**, tap **Import SIM Contacts.**

- To import from a vCard, click on a .vcf attachment in a message or email.

Chapter 23: Phone App

Answer a Call

Answer a call in three ways:

- Press the center button of your AirPods, tap  or drag the slider on the locked screen.
- Tap the mute button to mute the call.
- Press and hold the mute button to put the call on hold.
- Click the audio button, then select an audio destination to talk hands-free. Tap to end the call.

Announce Calls

The iPhone can announce all your incoming calls or just the calls that come in when using Bluetooth or headphones in your car.

- Go to Settings, tap **Phone,** then click **Announce Calls.**

Decline a Call

- Swipe up on the call banner, tap 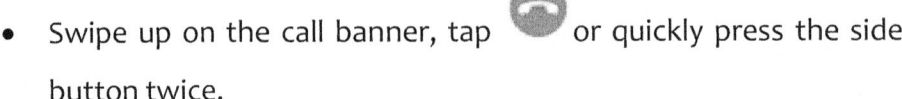 or quickly press the side button twice.

- To set a reminder to return the call, click **Remind Me,** and then choose the period you want to receive the reminder.

- To decline and reply with a message, click **Message,** then select a default response or click **Custom.**

- To silence the call, press the side or volume buttons once.

Create Default Reply

iPhone 12 has its default replies, but you can create your own replies.

- Go to Settings, tap **Phone,** then click **Respond with Text.**

- Click on an existing message and replace it with a new text.

Use Another App while on a Call

You can multitask while making or receiving a call.

- Go to the home screen and click an app to launch it.

- Tap the icon at the top of the screen to return to the call.

Start a Conference Call

Make a call with up to five participants. Note that conference call is not available for Wi-Fi calling or VoLTE.

- While on one call, click **Add Call** to initiate another one. Once the receiver responds to the call, click **Merge Calls** to merge the calls.

170

- To drop one person from a conference call, tap ⓘ beside the person, and select **End.**

- To add an incoming caller to the conference call, select **Hold Call + Answer,** then click **Merge Calls.**

- To talk privately with a single participant, tap ⓘ and select **Private** next to the person. Click **Merge Calls** to return to the conference call.

Use Wi-Fi Calling

Wi-Fi calling makes and receives calls using your Wi-Fi network. To set this up,

- Go to **Settings,** tap **Cellular,** and choose a line if using a Dual SIM iPhone.

- Select **Wi-Fi Calling,** then toggle on **Wi-Fi Calling on This iPhone.**

- Confirm or input your address for emergency services.

Add a Contact to Favorite

Add a contact to your favorite list for quick dialing.

- Click on a contact in the Phone app.

- Then tap **Add to Favorites.**

- Calls from your favorite contacts will always come in even when you turn on Do Not Disturb.

Save a Dialed Number

- Open the Phone app and tap **Keypad.**

- Input the number, then click on **Add Number.**

- Click on **Add to Existing Contact** and choose the existing contact, or click on **Create New Contact.**

Add a Recent Caller to Contacts

- Open the Phone app and tap **Recents.**

- Tap beside a number, click **Add to Existing Contact** to choose an existing contact or click **Create New Contact** to add a new contact.

Hide Duplicate Contacts

By default, if you have different contacts with the same name saved on your phone, these contacts will be automatically linked and shown as a single contact. However, you can manually link these contacts if they aren't linked automatically.

- Open the contacts app and click on one of the contacts.
- Tap **Edit,** then click on **Link Contacts.**
- Choose the other contact and then click on **Link.**

If the linked contacts have different last or first names, the names on each of the cards will not change, but you will see one name on the unified card. To choose the name that should show on the unified card,

- Click on one of the linked cards and then click on the name on that card. Then click on **Use this Name for Unified Card.**

Block Unwanted Callers

You can block FaceTime calls, Voice calls, and messages from certain people. There are two ways to block a contact

- Open the Phone app and click on **Recents, Favorites,** or **Voicemail.** Tap beside the contact or number you wish to block, then tap **Block this Caller.**

- Tap **Contacts** in the Phone app, click the contact you wish to block, then tap **Block This Caller.**

Manage Blocked Contacts

To view your blocked contacts or unblock a contact,

- Go to Settings, tap **Phone,** and click **Blocked Contacts.**

- Tap **Edit** to modify.

Send Spam Callers to Voicemail

Follow the steps below to send spam and unknown callers to voicemail

- Go to Settings, and tap **Phone.**

- Click **Silence Unknown Callers** to only receive notifications for incoming calls from your saved contacts, Siri suggestions, and numbers you called recently.

- Click **Call Blocking & Identification,** then toggle on **Silence Junk Callers** to mute calls identified by your carrier as fraud or potential scam.

- The calls will then be sent to voicemail.

Make Calls using Wi-Fi

Wi-Fi calling uses a Wi-Fi network to make and receive calls, particularly when your phone has a low cellular signal.

- Go to Settings and tap **Cellular.**

- If using a Dual SIM phone, select a line under **Cellular Plans.**

- Tap **Wi-Fi Calling,** then enable **Wi-Fi Calling on This iPhone.**

- Confirm or input your address for emergency services.

Note that you can enable Wi-Fi calling for all your SIMs if using a Dual SIM iPhone.

Chapter 24: Safari on iPhone

Use the Safari app to surf the web, add page icons to the Home screen for faster access, and add webpages to your reading list. If you logged into iCloud with the same Apple ID across all your devices, you could view and keep your history, bookmarks, and reading list updated on all the devices.

View Websites with Safari

- Open the Safari app on your phone and tap the text field at the top of your screen to enter a search term or web address.

- Double-click the top edge of your screen to quickly move from the bottom to the top of a long page.

- Switch your phone to landscape orientation to view more of the page.

- Tap ↻ beside the web address to refresh the page.

- Tap ⬆ at the bottom of the screen to share the web page.

You can turn off the option for searching within Safari,

- Go to **Settings,** tap **Safari,** then enable or disable **Quick Website Search.**

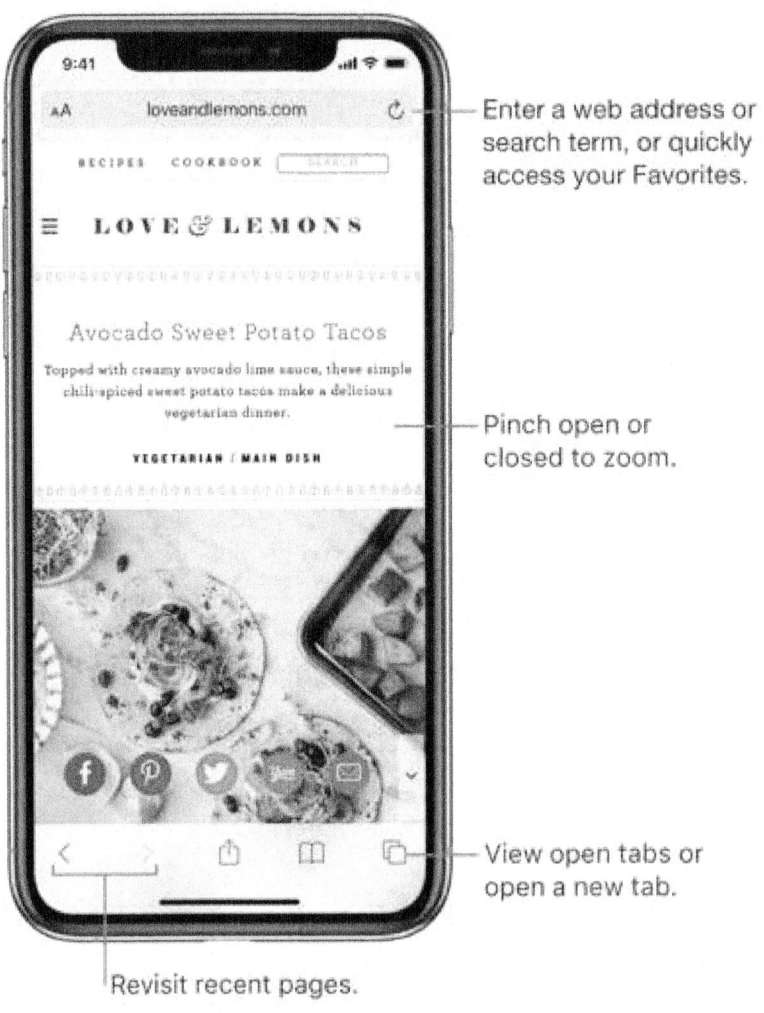

Enter a web address or search term, or quickly access your Favorites.

Pinch open or closed to zoom.

View open tabs or open a new tab.

Revisit recent pages.

Customize Website Settings

You can change the display and text size, choose privacy restrictions, switch to reader view, and so on from the View menu on Safari.

- Tap AA at the top left side of your screen to open the View menu.
- Click the smaller A to reduce the font size or bigger A to increase it.

- Click **Show Reader View** to browse the webpage without any navigation menus or ads.

- Tap **Hide Toolbar** to hide the search field. Tap the top of your screen to unhide.

- Tap **Request Desktop Website** for a desktop version of a webpage.

- Tap **Website Settings** to change the display and privacy controls for that website.

Erase Browsing History

- Go to Settings, tap **Safari,** then tap **Clear History and Website Data.**

Private Browsing

Go for private browsing if you do not want the system to store your browsing history.

- Open Safari, tap and then click **Private.**

- To exit Private browsing, tap and click **Private.**

Preview Website Link

You can preview a link without opening the page.

- Press down on a link in Safari to view a preview of the link.

- To open the link, tap the preview and choose an option on your screen.

- To exit the preview while staying on the current page, click any spot outside the preview.

Touch and hold a link to see the URL and these options.

Translate a Webpage

To translate a webpage from one language to another,

- Click AA on the page, then select 🗨.

Search the Page

To find a specific phrase or word on a page,

- Tap ⬆ at the bottom of the page, then click **Find on Page.**

- Type the phrase or word in the search field, then tap $\vee$ to find all the instances for that word.

Choose a Search Engine

To choose a default engine for searching on Safari,

- Go to **Settings,** tap **Safari,** and tap **Search Engine** to choose.

Open Link in a New Tab

you can open a link in a different tap or the current tab. You can also customize the new tabs to open in the background, rather than directing you straight to the new page.

- To open a link, hold the link and click **Open in New Tab.** Alternatively, click the link with two fingers.

To open the new tab in the background,

- Go to Settings, tap **Safari,** click **Open Links,** then select **In Background.**

Browse Open Tabs

- Tap ▢ at the bottom of your screen to see all your open tabs.

- Swipe left on a tab or tap ✕ at the top left corner to close a tab.

- To return to a single tab, click a tab or click **Done** to return to the current tab.

- To view a tab's history, press, and hold $<$ or $>$.

- To reopen a recently closed tab, tap ▢ , press and hold $+$, then select a tab from the list on your screen.

Bookmark the Current Page

Bookmark a webpage to quickly access it at any time.

- Press and hold , then click **Add Bookmark.**

- To view your bookmarks, tap and then click the Bookmarks tab.

- Tap **Edit** to create a new folder, rename, reorder or delete bookmarks.

Add a Webpage to Your Favorite

- Tap at the bottom of the page, then click **Add to Favorites.**

- To view and edit your favorites, tap , click the Bookmarks tab, click **Favorites,** then tap **Edit** to rearrange, rename or delete your favorites.

Stop Seeing Frequently Visited Sites

Open Safari & scroll down to view your frequently visited sites. But you can choose not to have your frequently visited sites on the Safari home page.

- Go to Settings, tap **Safari,** and disable **Frequently Visited Sites.**

Add Website Icon to Your Home Screen

You can add an icon for a website you often visit to your phone's home screen to quickly access the site in the future.

- Tap at the bottom of the page, then click **Add to Home Screen.**

Add and View Your Reading List

To add a page to your reading list,

- Tap ⬆️ at the bottom of the page, then click **Add to Reading List.**

- To add a link to the reading list without opening it, press firmly on the link and then choose **Add to Reading List.**

- Tap 📖 to view your reading list and then select ○○ .

- Swipe left on an item to remove it from your reading list.

You can also configure your phone to save your reading list automatically to iCloud for offline reading.

- Go to Safari, tap **Safari,** then enable **Automatically Save Offline.**

Automatically Fill in Your Contact Details

When you enter your contact details on a website that supports **AutoFill,** click **AutoFill Contact** on your keyboard to add the details to autofill. When next you need to fill in your contact details, you can tap **AutoFill** to complete the field automatically.

- Click **Customize** to modify and store your details for next time. Or click **Other Contact** to input another person's details.

Set up Credit Card for Purchases

To add a credit card for your purchases on Safari,

- Go to Safari, tap **Safari,** tap **Autofill,** and then click **Saved Credit Cards.**

- Tap **Add Credit Card** to set up a new card. Click **Use Camera** to use your phone camera to capture the card details. Else, enter the card manually.

- To use the card for payment, tap **Autofill Credit Card** above your keyboard, then enter the card's security code to complete.

Disable AutoFill

You can disable Autofill for your passwords or your credit/contact details. You will then need to input your contact and card details manually when requested by sites.

- To disable Autofill for credit/ contact details, Go to Settings, tap **Safari,** tap **Autofill,** and then disable any of the options.
- To disable Autofill for passwords, go to Settings, tap **Password,** then disable **Autofill Passwords.**

Hide Distractions and Ads

With the Reader view on Safari, you can hide ads and other distracting items. Reader View will only show the relevant text and images on a webpage.

- Open a webpage on Safari, then tap $A\!A$ at the top left side of your screen, and click **Show Reader View.**

- To go back to the full page, tap $A\!A$ and click **Hide Reader View.**

Note that Reader View isn't available on all pages.

Tap to view the
page in Reader.

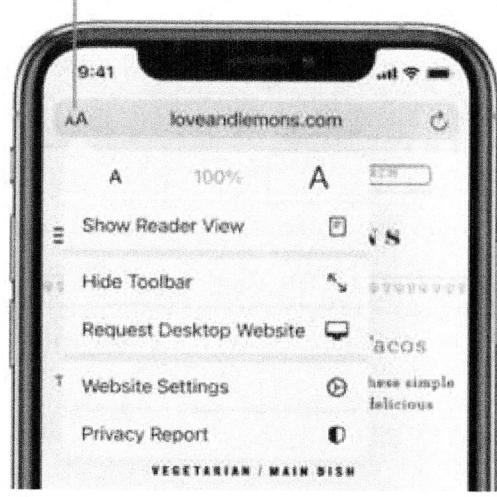

Automatically Use Reader View

To automatically switch to Reader View on supported websites,

- Open Safari, then tap **AA** at the top left.

- Click **Website Settings,** then enable **Use Reader Automatically.**

Block Pop-Ups

- Go to Settings, tap **Safari,** then enable **Block Pop-Ups.**

Chapter 25: The Reminders App

Create and organize reminders to stay organized and track your daily activities. Create subtasks, add attachments, set flags, and choose when you want to receive reminders.

Sync Your Reminders on All Your Devices
This option ensures that your reminders are up to date across all your devices.

- Go to Settings, tap your name, tap **iCloud,** and turn on **Reminders**

- Any change you make on one device will appear on other devices with the same Apple ID as the iPhone.

Add a Reminder
- Click **New Reminder** and enter your text.

- Tap to schedule a time and date – choose when you wish to be reminded.

- Tap to add a location – then select where you want to receive the reminder. For instance, when you get into a car with a Bluetooth connection to your iPhone or when you get home.

- Tap to assign the reminder to a contact – then select a contact on the shared list (this is available in shared lists).

- Tap to flag an important reminder.

- Tap to attach a scanned document or photo to a reminder.

To add more details to the reminder, click (i) and then

- Enter a web address in the URL field or enter more info about the reminder in the Notes field.

- To receive a reminder when chatting with someone in the Messages app, toggle on **When Messaging,** then select a contact.

- To set a priority, click **Priority** and select an option.

- Tap **Done** to finish.

Mark a Reminder as Complete
- Click the empty circle by the side of a reminder to mark it as complete – this will hide the reminder.

- To unhide completed reminders, tap (...) and choose **Show Completed.**

Edit Multiple Reminders at Once
- Tap (...), choose **Reminders** and then choose the reminders you want to edit.

- Use the buttons at the end of the screen to flag, move, complete, assign, delete, or add a date and time to the selected reminders.

Move or Delete Reminders
- Tap and hold a reminder, then move it to a new location.

- Create a subtask – swipe right on a reminder, then click **Index.** Or pull one reminder on top of another. When you move or delete a parent task, the subtasks are also moved or deleted. If you complete a parent task, it also affects the subtasks.

- To move a reminder to a different list, click on the reminder, tap

  (i) , select **List,** and then click on a list.

- Swipe left on a reminder to delete it – then select **Delete.** To recover a deleted reminder, double-tap with three fingers or shake to undo.

Create Reminder Lists and Groups

Organize your reminders into lists and groups of lists like shopping, school, or work.

- To create a new list, tap **Add List** at the bottom right, enter a name for your list, then choose a color and a symbol.

- To create a group of lists, click **Edit** at the top, select **Add Group,** choose a name, and select **Create.** Another way to create a group is to drag one list on the top of another list.

- To reorder and move lists, tap and hold a list, then pull it to a new location or drop in a different group.

- To edit a group or a list, swipe left on the list, then tap (i) .

- To delete a group or list, swipe left and tap 🗑 .

Change Your Reminder Settings

- Go to Settings, tap **Reminders.**

- Click **Accounts** to add an account like Microsoft, iCloud, etc.

- Tap **Today Notification** to select a time to show notifications for all-day reminders that do not have a specified time.

- Tap **Default List** to create a list for new reminders that are not created within a specific list.

- Tap **Mute Notifications** to disable notifications for selected reminders.

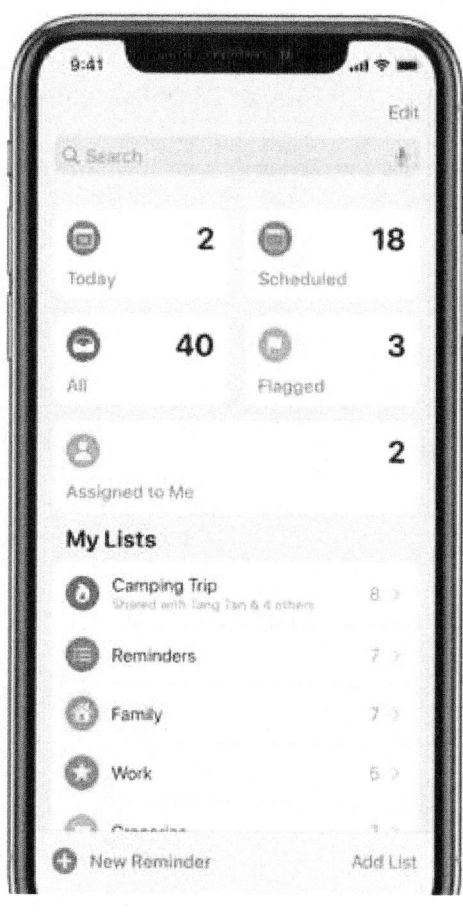

Use Smart Lists
Use Smart Lists to organize and track upcoming reminders automatically.

- Below the search field, tap **Today** to see your today's reminders as well as your overdue reminders.

- Tap **Scheduled** to view reminders scheduled by time or date.

- Tap **Flagged** to view all your flagged reminders.

- Tap **Assigned to Me** to view the reminders assigned to you.

- Tap **Siri Suggestions** to view Siri suggested reminders detected in Messages and Mail.

- Tap **All** to view all your reminders across every list.

- Tap **Edit** at the top of the screen to hide, show, or rearrange the smart lists.

Share a List Using iCloud

Share and collaborate with other iCloud users. Once the receiver accepts the invite, they can add and edit reminders or mark reminders as completed.

- Open a list, tap ⊙ and select **Share List.**

- Then select a sharing method, e.g., Messages or Mail.

Assign Reminders in a Shared List

Assign a reminder to any member of a list, including yourself.

- Click the desired reminder and tap 👤.

- Then select a person on the shared list.

Chapter 26: Camera App

Take a Photo

- Open the Camera app on your home screen or swipe left from your lock screen to launch the camera in Photo mode.

- Tap to use or not use flash. Or tap and then click below the frame to choose between **On, Off,** or **Auto.**

- To set a timer for the photo, tap then click.

- Press any of the volume buttons or tap the Shutter button to take a shot.

Take a Selfie

- Open the Camera and tap or to switch to the front camera.

- Position your phone in front of you. You may also click the arrows inside the frame to increase the field of view.

- Tap any of the volume buttons or the shutter button to capture your photo.

Mirror Front Camera

Another way to take a selfie is to take a mirrored selfie. The Mirrored selfie snaps a photo that's like your mirror image as if you are staring at the mirror. You will see the image as you see yourself in the mirror. To turn it on,

- Go to Settings, tap **Camera,** then toggle on **Mirror Front Camera.**

Adjust the Camera's Exposure and Focus

When you open the Camera app to take a photo, the app automatically sets the exposure and focus of the camera lens, and face detection balances the exposures across the faces in the viewfinder. To manually adjust the exposure and focus,

- Click your screen to view the automatic focus area and exposure setting.
- Click on the area you want the focus on.

- Drag the ⛯ icon next to the focus area up or down to adjust the exposure.

- To lock your manual exposure and focus settings and use it for upcoming shots, tap and hold the focus area until the AE/AF lock appears. Click the screen to unlock the settings.

Take a Live Photo

Live Photos capture what happens a few seconds before and after you capture your photo. To take a Live Photo,

- Open the Camera app and stay on Photo mode.

- Tap ◎ to turn on **Live Photos,** then click the Shutter button to capture your photo.

Use Night Mode

Night mode captures more detail and brightens the photos you take in low-light situations. The phone automatically turns on Night mode in low-light situations. If the ⬤ button at the top of the viewfinder turns yellow, it means that night mode is on. A number then appears beside the button, indicating how many seconds before the camera will take a shot.

- Click the Shutter button, then hold your phone still to capture your shot.

- To customize before taking a shot, tap the ⬤ button, then pull the slider to choose between Max and Auto timers. The auto timer automatically sets the time while Max uses the longest time.

191

- Tap the Stop button below the slider to stop taking a night mode shot mid-capture.

Panorama Mode

Use this mode to capture landscapes or other shots that may not fit on your camera viewfinder.

- Open the Camera app and swipe to Pano mode.
- Click the Shutter button to start shooting, then pan or turn your device to capture your surroundings. Ensure that the point of the arrow stays in line with the yellow guide on your screen.
- Rotate your phone to landscape orientation to pan vertically or tap the arrow to pan in the opposite direction.
- Tap the Shutter button again to stop recording.

Take a Photo with a Filter

To apply filters to your photos,

- Open the Camera app, tap , then click .
- You will find the filters below the viewer. Swipe through the different filters and tap one to use it.

Take Burst Shots

Use a burst shot to capture a series of images in rapid succession. It's a great way to shoot a fast-moving object/ scene, an action scene, or an unexpected event. It gives you several photos to choose from.

- Swipe the Shutter button to the left, then hold the shutter to take your burst shots. The counter will display how many shots you took.

- Lift your finger to stop shooting.

- Tap the image thumbnail at the bottom left side of your screen to view the photos. To choose photos, tap **Select,** then choose the photos you wish to save and tap **Done** to save them.

- To delete the complete Burst shot, click the thumbnail, then click

Use Volume Up for Burst

You can press down the volume up button to capture your burst shots. To set this up,

- Go to Settings, tap **Camera,** then enable **Use Volume up for Burst.**

Record a Video

- Open the camera app and swipe to Video mode.
- Tap any of the volume buttons or tap the Record button to start recording.
- Press the white shutter button to take a photo while recording.
- Pinch your screen to zoom out or in.
- Tap any of the volume buttons or tap the Record button to stop recording.

Customize Video Resolution Settings

By default, the iPhone records videos at 30 frames per second. However, you can choose the frame rate of your choice and also change your video resolution settings,

- Go to Settings, tap **Camera,** tap **Record Video,** and choose your preferred frame rate.
- To record 4k video, select either 4K at 30fps or 4K at 60fps option. If you selected 4k at 30fps, you could also toggle on **Auto-Low Light Fps** to automatically reduce the frame rate from 30 to 24 to improve low-light videos.

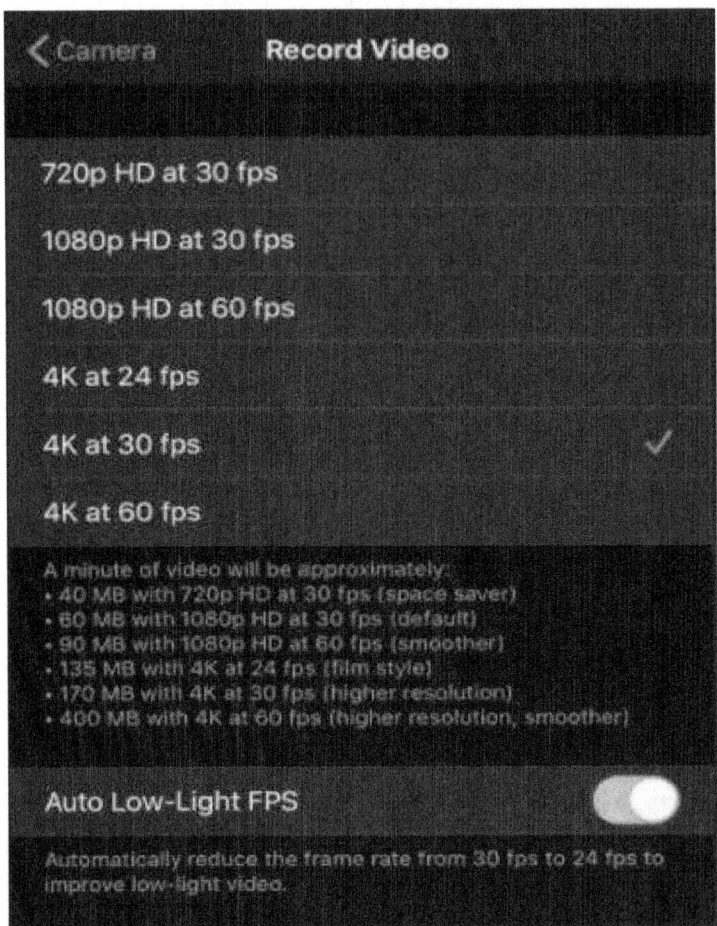

Record Stereo Sound

iPhone automatically uses multiple microphones to achieve the stereo sound. The stereo sound helps your video to sound better. To turn it on or off,

- Go to Settings, tap **Camera,** enable or disable **Record Stereo Sound.**

Quickly Change Frame Rate and Video Resolution

While in Video mode, you can use the quick toggles to choose frame rates and video resolution rate.

- Click the quick toggles at the upper right side of your camera viewfinder to switch between 4K or HD recording and 24,30 or 60 frames per second.

Record Quick Take Video

You can quickly take a video while in the Photo mode.

- Open the camera app and stay on Photo mode.
- Tap and hold the shutter button to begin recording your video.

- Slide the shutter button to the right and release it over the lock to record hands-free.

- Tap the shutter button to capture a photo while recording, then tap the Record button to stop recording.

- Click the thumbnail at the bottom left to view your video.

Tip: tap and hold any of the volume buttons while in Photo mode to start recording your QuickTake video.

Record Slow-mo Video

The Slow-mo video records as usual, but the slow-mo effect kicks in when you playback the video. You can also edit the video to limit the slow-motion action to a specified area in the video.

- Open the camera and swipe to Slow-mo mode. Tap to record Slow-mo videos using the front camera.

- Press any of the volume buttons or tap the Record button to start recording. Tap any of the buttons again to stop recording. Tap the shutter button to capture a photo while recording.

You can also change the frame rate and resolution for slow-motion videos:

- Go to Settings, tap **Camera,** then tap **Record Slo-mo.**

Capture a Time-Lapse Video

Use the Time-Lapse video mode to capture different footages at selected intervals to get a time-lapse video of an experience over a certain period – like traffic flowing or a setting sun.

- Open the camera and swipe to **Time-Lapse** mode.

- Set your phone on a tripod to get the best result.

- Click the Record button to begin recording and tap the button again to stop recording.

- Toggle between 1× and 2× to zoom in on the scene or tap 0.5× to zoom out.

Portrait Mode

Portrait mode allows you to take a photo that focuses on the subject while blurring the background. The subject's face will be perfectly sharp while the background of the photo will be beautifully blurred.

- Open the camera and swipe to **Portrait** mode.

- Follow the tips on your screen to fit the subject into the yellow portrait box.

- Drag the icon to select a lighting effect:

  ➢ **Studio Light:** brightly lits the face and gives the photo an overall clean look.

  ➢ **Natural Light:** focuses on the face while blurring the background.

  ➢ **Contour Light:** gives the face dramatic shadows with lowlights and highlights.

  ➢ **Stage Light:** makes a face spotlit against a deep black background.

  ➢ **Stage Light Mono:** similar effect as Stage Light, but the photo is in classic white and black.

  ➢ **High-Key Light Mono:** gives a grayscale subject on a white background.

- Click the Shutter button  to capture your image.

Adjust Depth Control in Portrait Mode

The Depth control slider allows you to adjust the level of background blur in the photos you take on Portrait mode.

- Open the camera and swipe to **Portrait** mode.

- Tap ⓕ at the top right, and you will see the slider below the frame.

- Drag the slider left and right to adjust the effect, then tap the Shutter button to take your photo.

Adjust Portrait Lighting Effects in Portrait Mode

When taking a Portrait mode photo, you can adjust each Portrait Lighting effect's intensity and position to sharpen the eyes or smoothen and brighten the subject's facial features.

- Open the camera and swipe to **Portrait** mode.

- Drag the ⬡ icon to select a lighting effect, then tap ⬢ at the top of your screen to bring up the Portrait lighting slider below the frame.

- Drag the slider left and right to adjust the effect, then tap the Shutter button to take your photo.

Align Your Shot

You can set up the camera app to show a grid on your screen that you can use to straighten your shots. To turn on this grid,

- Go to Settings, tap **Camera,** then enable **Grid.**

Preserve Camera Settings

You can save your last camera mode, depth, filter, lighting, and Live Photo Settings that you used to be available when next you launch the camera.

- Go to Settings, tap **Camera,** then tap **Preserve Settings.**

- Turn on **Camera Mode** to preserve the last camera mode you used.

- Turn on **Creative Controls** to preserve the last lighting, filter option, or depth setting you used.

- Turn on **Exposure Adjustment** to preserve your exposure control setting.

- Turn on **Live Photo** to preserve the existing Live Photo setting.

Adjust the Shutter Sound Volume

To control the shutter sound volume, press the volume buttons on your iPhone. Another way to control the volume is below:

- Open the camera app and swipe down from the upper right corner of your screen. Then drag .

Note that you will not hear any shutter sound when using Live Photo mode.

Prioritize Faster Shooting

The prioritize faster shooting setting alters how images are processed. This setting helps you to shoot even faster when you rapidly tap the shutter button. The setting is enabled by default. To disable,

- Go to Settings, tap **Camera,** then disable **Prioritize Faster Shooting.**

Customize View Content Outside the Frame

The camera preview on the iPhone 12 displays content outside of the frame to show users other things you can capture using another lens in the camera system. If you do not like this feature, you can turn it off here,

- Go to Settings, tap **Camera,** then disable **View Outside the Frame.**

Turn Off Automatic HDR

HDR (High Dynamic Range) refers to the way images are processed. The setting gives you great shots in high contrast situation. The iPhone automatically uses HDR when it thinks it is needed. If you wish to control HDR manually,

- Go to **Settings,** tap **Camera,** and then turn off **Smart HDR.** Then you can tap **HDR** in the camera screen to manually turn it on or off.

View Your Photos

You can view your photos right after shooting them:

- Click the thumbnail image at the bottom left corner of your screen.

- Swipe right or left to view your recently shot photos.

- Click on the screen to show or hide the controls.

- Click **All Photos** to view all the videos and photos saved in Photos.

Read a QR Code

To use your phone to read a QR code

- Open the camera, then place your phone so that the code shows on the screen.

- Click the notification on your screen to go to the app or website.

Open QR Code Reader from Control Center

Asides the Camera app, you can also open the QR code reader from the control center:

- Go to Settings, tap **Control Center,** then click ⊕ beside **QR Code Reader.**

- Open Control Center on your phone, click the QR code reader, then place your phone so that the code shows on the screen.

- Click the notification on your screen to go to the app or website.

Chapter 27: Photos App

The Photos app organizes your videos and photos by days, months, years, and all Photos. Click the **Search, Albums,** or **For You** tab to find photos organized by individual categories and create albums that you can share with friends and family.

- Click the Library tab to browse through your videos and photos organized into days, months, and years.

- Click the Albums tab to view the albums you shared or created. You will also see your photos organized by album categories like **People & Places.**

- Click **For You** to view a personalized feed showing photos you featured in, your shared albums, your memories, and more.

- Click the **Search** tab to search for photos using caption, location, date, or objects they contain.

Browse Photos
To view your videos and photos by Months, Days, Years, or All Photos,

- Open the Photos app and click the Library tab.

- Then click **Days, Months, Years,** or **All Photos** depending on what you want to see.

- Tap the icon to play a movie, filter photos, share photos, or see a photo on a map.

Tap to share, play movie, and see location on a map.

Tap to view full screen.

- Click on a photo to explode in full screen, then tap ⬆️ to share the photo or tap ♡ to add the photo to your Favorites.

- Pinch or double-tap to zoom in, or pinch closed or double-tap to zoom out.

- To return to All Photos or the search results, tap ‹ or drag the photo down.

Play a Live Photo

Live Photos capture events that happen a few seconds before and after you capture your photo. To play a live Photo,

- Open the Live Photo, then touch and hold the Photo to play.

View Photos in a Burst Shot
Each Burst shots images is captured in one single photo thumbnail. You can then view all the photos in a Burst and choose the ones you want to save individually.

- Open a Burst Photo and click **Select.**

- Swipe through the photos in the collection, tap a photo(s) to choose it, then click **Done.**

- Click **Keep Everything** to keep the Burst shots and the photos you selected. Or, click **Keep Only (number of) Favorites** to save only the photos you selected.

Play a Video
While browsing through your photos in the Library tab, you will see your videos auto-play.

- Click on a video to play it in full screen without sound, then tap the player controls below the video to play, pause, mute and unmute.

- Tap the screen again to hide the player controls.

- Double click your screen to toggle between fit-to-screen and full screen.

Create a Slideshow

A slideshow brings your photos together, adds music, themes, etc. and then converts them into a video. To create a slideshow:

- Click the **Library** tab, select **Days** or **All Photos,** then click **Select.**

- Click all the photos you want in the slideshow, then click ⬆️.

- Click **Slideshow** from the options on your screen.

- Tap your screen, then click **Options** in the bottom right of your screen to change the slideshow music, theme, and more.

Hide and Delete Photos and Videos

- Open a video or photo, then tap 🗑 at the bottom to delete.

- To hide it, click ⬆ and then click **Hide.**

- Deleted content is kept in the **Recently Deleted** album for 30 days before they are permanently removed from the device.

- Hidden photos are stored in the Hidden album.

Permanently Delete or Recover Deleted Photos

You can recover deleted photos and videos up to 30 days after they are deleted. To permanently delete these content before 30 days or recover them,

- Click the **Albums** tab, click **Recently Deleted,** then tab **Select.**

- Choose the content you want to delete or recover, then click **Delete** or **Recover** at the bottom of your screen.

Edit Your Photos and Videos

- Click on a video or photo to open it in full screen.

- Tap **Edit,** then swipe left under the image to view the editing buttons for each effect like **Highlights, Brilliance,** and **Exposure.**

- Click each button, then pull the slider to adjust the effect.

- To review the changes, click the effect button to see the original image and the edited image or click the photo to toggle between the original and the edited version.

- Tap **Done** to accept the changes or tap **Cancel,** then click **Discard Changes.**

Tip: tap the  icon under the Photo to edit your videos or photos automatically with effects.

Rotate, Flip, or Crop

- Open the photo, and tap **Edit.**

- To crop, tap ⬚ then drag the rectangle corners to select just the parts of the photo you want, or pinch the photo open or closed to crop the photo or video. To crop to a standard preset ratio, click

![icon] and choose a ratio. Tap ![icon] to rotate the photo 90 degrees.

- Tap ![icon] to flip the image horizontally.

- Tap **Done** to accept the changes or tap **Cancel,** then click **Discard**

  Changes.

Apply Filter

You can always add or remove filters from your photos or videos

- Open the video or photo, and tap **Edit.**

- Tap ![icon] to display the filter effects such as Dramatic, Vivid, and

  more.

- Click a filter, then drag the slider to use the filter on your content.

- Click the photo to compare the original and edited versions.

- Tap **Done** to accept the changes or tap **Cancel,** then click **Discard**

  Changes.

Straighten and Adjust your Photos

You can straighten or adjust the perspectives for your photo.

- Open the photo, and tap **Edit.**

- Tap ![icon] and choose an effect button to adjust the horizontal or

  vertical perspective or straighten the photo.

- Drag the slider under the Photo to adjust each effect. Any adjustment

  you make on the image will be displayed by the yellow outline around

  the button to help you see in one glance, the effects that you included. Click the button to switch between the original and edited effect.

Drag to tilt or straighten.

- Tap **Done** to accept the changes or tap **Cancel,** then click **Discard Changes.**

Mark up a Photo

You can write, draw or annotate your photos with the steps below

- Open the photo and tap **Edit.** Tap ⬤ , then tap **Markup** Ⓐ.

- Use the drawing tools and colors on your screen to annotate the photo—tap ➕ to include text, shape, or signature.

Trim a Video

You can make a long video shorter with the steps below:

- Open the video and tap **Edit.**

- Drag either end of the frame viewer to choose the start and end points for the video, then tap **Done.**

- Click **Save Video** to keep only the trimmed video or click **Save Video as New Clip** to keep both versions of your video.

Revert an Edited Photo/ Video

You can always return an edited photo or video to its original version.

- Open the edited photo or video, and tap **Edit.**

- Tap **Revert,** then click **Revert to Original.**

Note that you would be unable to revert to the original version for a video you saved as a new clip.

Edit Slow-Mo Videos

You can edit a slow-motion video to play a portion in slow motion and the rest at regular speed. To do this,

- Click the video thumbnail after capturing the video or in the Photo app, then tap **Edit.**

- Use the white vertical bars under the frame viewer to select the section that should playback in slow motion.

Edit a Live Photo

You can trim the length, change the Key Photo, or mute the sound in your Live Photos.

- Open the Live Photo and click **Edit.**

- Click ⊚ then do any of the following:

  ✓ To trim a live photo, drag the ends of the frame viewer to choose the frames you want Live Photo to play.

  ✓ To turn off Live Photo, click the **Live** button at the top of your screen. Click it again to turn on Live Photo.

  ✓ Tap 🔊 at the top of your screen to mute a Live Photo. Tap again to unmute.

  ✓ To choose a key photo, move the white frame on your frame viewer to the desired frame, click **Make Key Photo,** and click **Done.**

Add Effects to a Live Photos

You can convert your Live Photos into fun videos. There are three special effects you can apply to a Live Photo to make it fun: Bounce, Loop and Long Exposure.

- Open the Live Photo and swipe up to view the available effects.
- Click on the effects you want to apply it to your photo or tap **Live** to revert to the original photo.
    - ✓ **Loop**: this turns your Live Photo into a continuous looping video. Once the video ends, it automatically begins playing from the beginning again until you stop it—best for when the

subject is repeating the same thing like juggling, dancing or skipping.

- ✓ **Bounce:** rewinds the action backward and forward until you stop it.
- ✓ **Long Exposure:** gives your photo a long exposure effect by blurring the motion.

Edit Portrait Images

After capturing a photo in Portrait mode, you can remove the Portrait mode effect in the photo, add or remove lighting effect to your image.

- Open the Portrait photo.

- Tap **Edit,** and click **Portrait** at the top of your screen to turn off the Portrait effect. Tap it again to turn it on.

- The lighting effect appears at the bottom of the image. Swipe through the lighting to choose the one you like. Then tap **Done** to save your changes.

Adjust Depth Control in Portrait Mode

The Depth control slider allows you to adjust the level of background blur in the photos you take on Portrait mode.

- Open the Portrait photo and tap **Edit.**

- Tap  at the top right, and you will see the slider below the frame.

- Drag the slider left and right to adjust the effect, then tap **Done** to save the changes.

Create an Album
Create an album to keep your Photos organized.

- Click the **Albums** tab and then click ✛.

- Select either **New Shared Album** (to share with friends and family) or **New Album.**

- Enter a name for the album, then click **Save.**

- Select the videos and photos to add to the album and then click **Done.**

To add videos and photos to an existing album,

- Click the Library tab and then click **Select.**

- Click the video and photos you want to add, then click ⬆.

- Swipe up, then click **Add to Album** or **Add to Shared Album,** then choose the album.

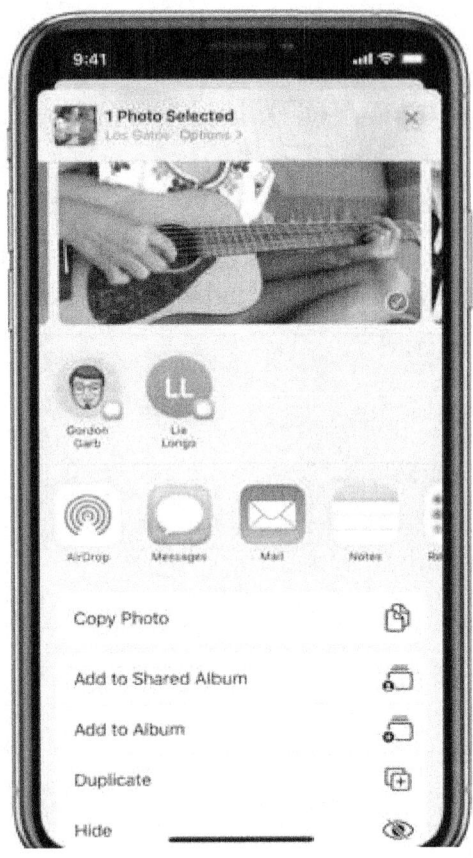

Remove Videos and Photos from an Album

- Open the album and click on the video or photo to view it in full screen.

- Tap 🗑 and then choose to remove the photo from the album or delete it from all your linked devices.

Edit an Album

To rearrange, rename or delete existing albums,

- Click the Albums tab, click **See All,** and then tap **Edit.**

- To rename, click the album name and input a new name.

- To delete, tap ⊖ .

- To rearrange, touch and hold the thumbnail for the album, then drag it to a different location.

- Tap **Done** to save.

To sort photos in an album,

- Select the album, tap ••• then click **Sort.**

Share and Print Your Photos

To share or print,

- Open the photo and tap ⬆️ .

- Choose an option to share the photo – like Messages, AirDrop, or Mail.

- Swipe up and choose **Print** if you wish to print your photo.

Chapter 28: Health and Fitness

Use the Health app on your iPhone to track the flight of stairs you climb daily and your daily footsteps. You can also manually input other details like your caffeine intake and body weight.

Manually Update Your Health Profile

The first time you launch the Health app, you will see a notification to set up a health profile. If you did not provide all the requested data, you could follow the steps below to do it later.

- Open the Health app and tap your initials or profile picture at the top right. If this isn't showing, tap **Browse** or **Summary** at the bottom of your screen, then move to the top.

- Click **Health Details,** then click **Edit** at the top right.

- Tap a field, enter the requested detail, and then tap **Done.**

Manually Add Data to a Health Category

To enter your health data,

- Open the Health app and click the **Browse** tab at the bottom of your screen.

- Click on a category, scroll down to see all categories. Or use the search field to search for a category.

- Click ⟩ for the data you want to modify.

- Click **Add Data** at the upper-right part of your screen, enter your details, then click **Done** or **Add** at the top of your screen.

View Your Health and Fitness Details

The Health app shows your health and fitness information. To view your highlights,

- Open the Health app and click the **Summary** tab.

- Tap ⟩ beside a category to view more details about that category.

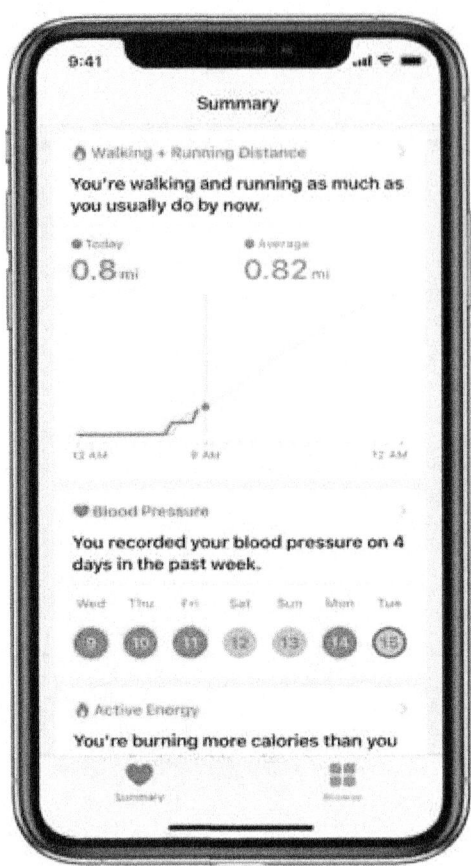

Remove or Add a Health Category to Favorites

The categories you add to Favorite will show at the top of the Health app.

- Open the Health app and click the **Summary** tab.

- Click **'Edit'** for the **Favorites** section, select a category to add or remove it.

- Then click **Done.**

View Details in the Health Categories

- Open the Health app and click the **Browse** tab.

- Scroll through the categories and click one to view the details on that category. Or use the search field to find a category.

- To further explode on any data in the selected category, tap the ＞ icon beside the data. You may then be able to edit or modify the details in the data that you exploded on:

    ➢ Click the tabs at the top of your screen to see the views of the data.

    ➢ Tap **Add Data** to enter information for that data manually.

    ➢ Toggle on **Add to Favorites** to add the data type to Favorites.

    ➢ Click **Data Sources & Access** below **Options** to view the devices and apps allowed to share data. Scroll down if the Options section isn't on your screen.

➢ To delete data, click **Show All Data,** then swipe left on a data record, and then select **Delete.** To delete all data, tap **Edit,** then click **Delete All.**

➢ To modify the measurement unit, click **Unit,** then select an option.

Connect to your Health Providers

Connect to your health provider to see your health records and get updates on your phone whenever you have a new entry from your health provider.

• Tap your initials or profile picture at the top of your screen, or tap the **Browse** or **Summary** tab, then click your profile picture.

• Click **Health Records,** then tap **Get Started** to set up your first health records.

• Tap **Add Account** to add another account if you already added one before.

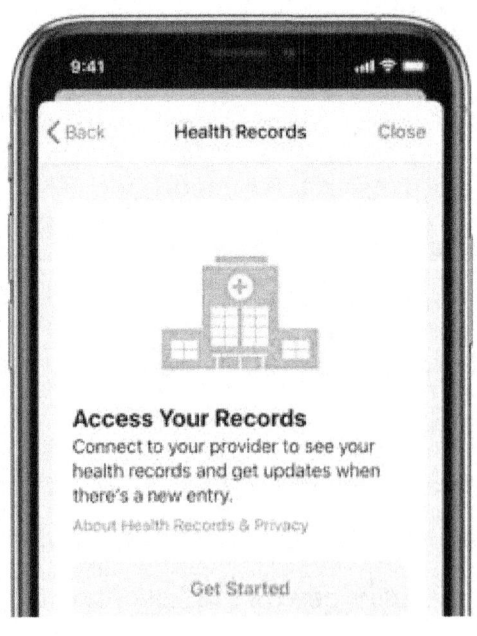

- Input the name of an organization that supplies your health record, like a hospital or clinic. Or enter the name of a state or city to see a list of the health organizations in that area. Tap a result to open.

- Scroll to **Available to Connect** and click the **Connect to Account** option to go to the patient portal's sign-in screen.

- Input your user name and password for the patient portal and proceed with the instructions on your screen.

View Your Health Records

- Click the **Browse** tab in the Health app.

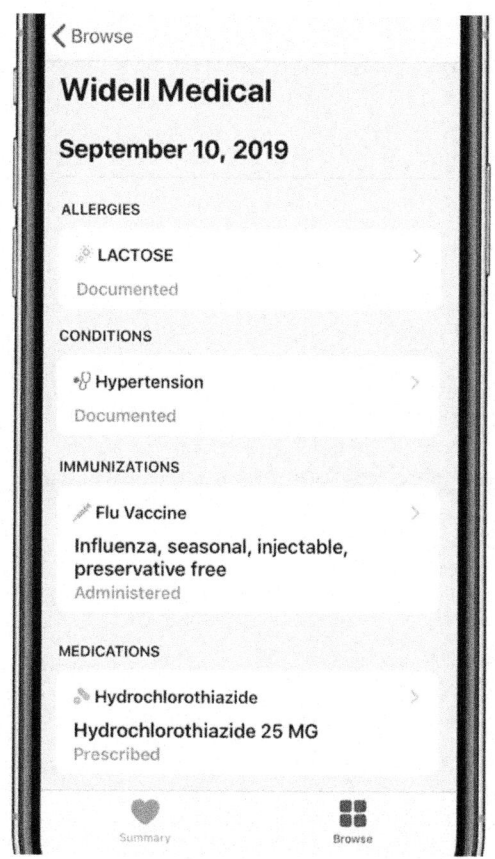

- Click the search field and input the name of a type of data like Blood Pressure or a health record category like Clinical Vitals.

- Scroll through the list and select a category under **Health Records.**

- Scroll down and click the name of an organization to view your record for that organization.

- Click on a section that has the $\diagup$ icon to view more details about that section.

Customize Notification Settings for Health Records

To get a notification when you have new data in your Health Records,

- Go to Settings, tap **Notifications,** click **Health,** then select your preference.

Delete an Organization and its Record

- Open the Health app and tap your initials or profile picture.

- Tap **Health Records,** select the organization, and tap **Remove Account.**

Control the Apps and Devices that can share Your Health Data

Use this setting to modify the apps and devices that can access and share your health data:

- Open the Health app and tap your initials/ profile picture at the top.

- Tap **Devices** or **Apps** under **Privacy.**

- The next screen will show you all the items that have access to your Health data.

- To change access for an app or device, tap the item, then enable or disable permission to read data from or write data to the Health app.

Create Your Medical ID

- Open the Health app and tap your initials/ profile picture at the top.

- Click **Get Started** to create your Medical ID/ tap **Edit** to change the ID.

- Turn on **Share During Emergency Call** to share your Medical ID data to emergency services when you use Emergency SOS or contact 911. This service is only available in the US.

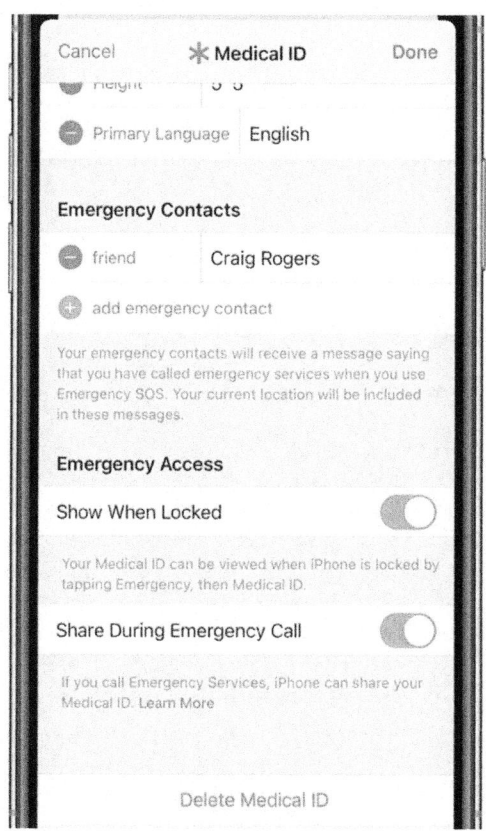

- Toggle on **Show When Locked** to enable first responders to view your Medical ID when your phone is locked. To access this, they will swipe up on your screen, tap **Emergency,** then tap **Medical ID.**

Here is how to quickly view your Medical ID:

- Go to the home screen, press firmly on the Health app icon, then select **Medical ID.**

Use the Health Checklist

Go through the health checklist to review and enable important features for the Health app:

- Open the Health app and tap your initials/ profile picture at the top.
- Click **Health Checklist,** click on an item to turn it on, or learn more about it.
- Tap **Back** to return to the checklist, then tap **Done** to finish.

Stop Storing Your Health Data in iCloud

Sharing your health data in iCloud ensures that all your linked devices are updated on your Health Information. To stop,

- Go to **Settings,** tap your name, tap **iCloud,** then disable **Health.**

Export and Share Your Health Data

- Tap your initials or profile picture at the top of your screen.
- Select **Export All Health Data,** then choose your sharing method.

Chapter 29: Cycle Tracking

You can track your cycle, get predictions on your fertile window, add symptoms, and lots more in the Health app.

- Open the Health app and click the **Browse** tab.
- Tap **Cycle Tracking,** click **Get Started,** then proceed with the instructions on your screen.
- Enter the requested details about your last period to get better predictions about your fertility and period window.

Log Your Cycle Information

To enter details about your monthly cycle,

- Open the Health app and click the **Browse** tab.
- Tap **Cycle Tracking,** then do any of the following:
  - ➢ Click a day in the timeline at the top of your screen to log a period day. To enter the flow level for that day, click **Period** under **Cycle Log,** then choose an option. Or click **Add Period** and then choose the days from the calendar. Click on a logged day to remove it.
  - ➢ To log symptoms, pull the timeline at the top of your screen to choose a day, click **Symptoms,** then choose all that applies. Tap **Done** to save.
  - ➢ To log spotting, pull the timeline to choose a day, click **Spotting,** select **Had Spotting,** then click **Done.**
- You can also add new categories like basal body temperature and ovulation test results. To do this, tap **Options,** then select the new category.

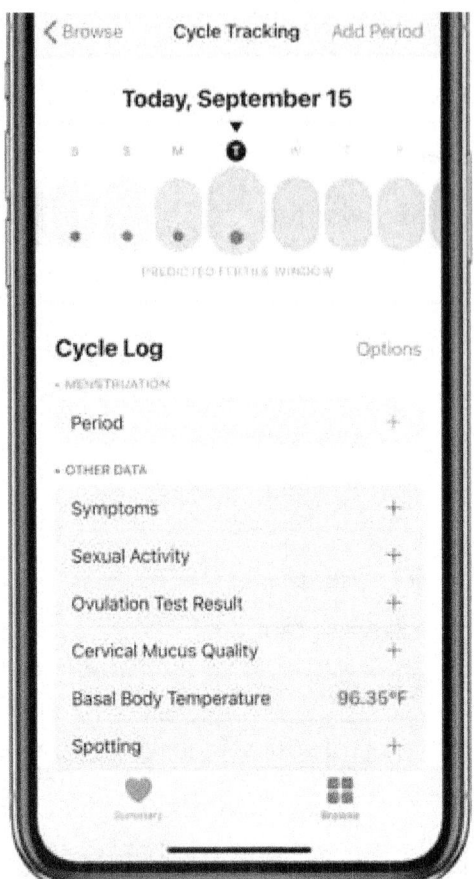

View Cycle Timeline

To view the days that you had your menstrual flow in the past,

- Click the **Browse** tab, then select **Cycle Tracking**.

- The solid red circles are the days you logged for your period, purple dot for days you entered symptoms, light red circles for your period prediction, and light blue days for fertility window prediction.

- Drag the timeline to view data for different days.

- To hide or show period prediction/ fertility prediction, click **Options,** then enable or disable **Period Prediction** and **Fertility Prediction.**

Adjust Fertility and Period Notifications

To customize your notifications for period and fertility predictions,

- Click the **Browse** tab, then select **Cycle Tracking**.

- Tap **Options** and then click on an option to enable or disable.

View Your Cycle History and Statistics

- Click the **Browse** tab, then select **Cycle Tracking**.

- Move down to see timelines for your last three recorded periods. Scroll further to view related statistics.

- For more details and older information for **Statistics** or **Cycle History,** tap ⟩ beside each section.

Chapter 30: Audio and Sound Level Exposure in Health

From the Health app, you can tell if your environment's sound is unhealthy for your hearing health. The app also spools record from your paired Apple Watch to notify you when the sound in the environment is unhealthy. From the Health app, you can also view a report that shows the average sound level in your environment within a specified period.

View Audio and Sound Level Exposure Information

The steps below will help you know whether sounds in your environment is too loud for your hearing health or not.

- Open the Health app and tap the **Browse** tab.

- Click **Hearing,** click **Environmental Sound Levels** or **Headphone Audio Levels,** then do any of the following:

  ➢ Tap (i) to learn about the sound level classifications.

  ➢ Click the tabs at the top of your screen to view your exposure levels over a period.

  ➢ Swipe the graph right or left to change the period shown in the graph.

  ➢ Tap and hold the graph, then drag to see details about a moment in time.

  ➢ To see details about your average exposure, click **Show All Filters,** then click **Daily Average.**

  ➢ Click **Exposure** under the graph to see a line representing average exposure.

➤ To view the different ranges, click **Show All Filters,** then click **Range.**

➤ To show the data for just the headphones, click **Show All Filters,** then select the headphones at the bottom of your screen.

➤ To see all the highlights, tap **Show All.**

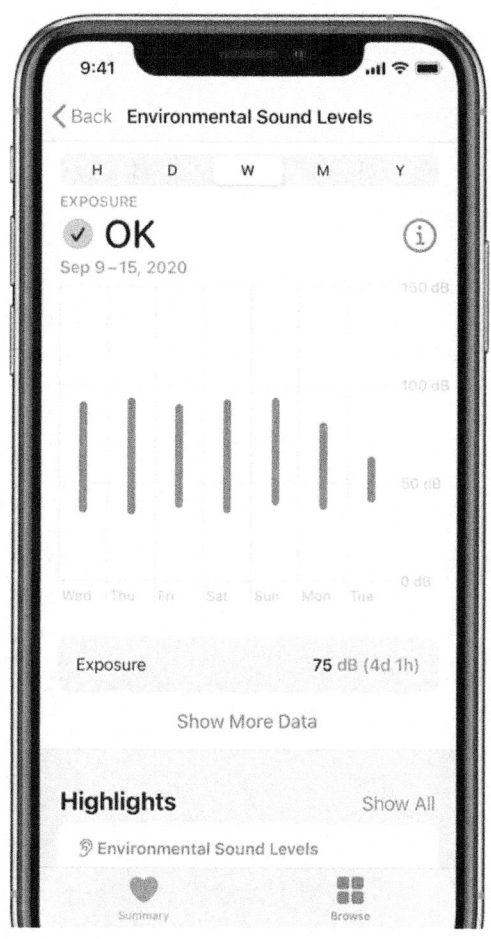

View Noise Notifications for Environmental Sounds

Sounds above 80 decibels are considered unhealthy for your ears. If you have a paired Apple Watch, you can choose to receive a notification from the watch when your environment's sound gets to an unhealthy level.

- Click the **Browse** tab, then select **Hearing**.
- Click **Noise Notification,** then click a notification to view more details.

Chapter 31: Monitor Your Sleep

You can use the Health app to set up a sleep schedule to wind down, wake up, and go to bed. Winding Down includes activities you do just before you sleep.

Set up Your First Sleep Schedule

To set up a schedule,

- Click the **Browse** tab, then select **Sleep**.

- Swipe up to **Set up Sleep,** and tap **Get Started,** then proceed with the instructions on your screen.

Change the Next Alarm

You can temporarily change your sleep schedule on a one-time basis.

- Click the **Browse** tab, then select **Sleep**.

- Scroll to **Your Schedule,** and tap **Edit.**

- To change your schedule for waking up and going to bed, drag 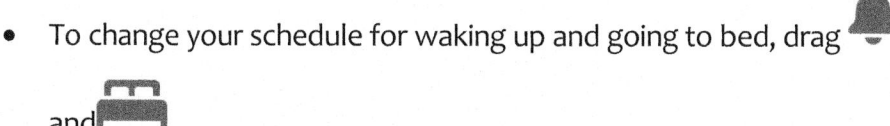 and .

- Toggle **Wake up Alarm** off or on, choose a sound and adjust the sound volume.

- Tap **Done** to save your changes.

- Your regular schedule resumes after the next wake-up alarm.

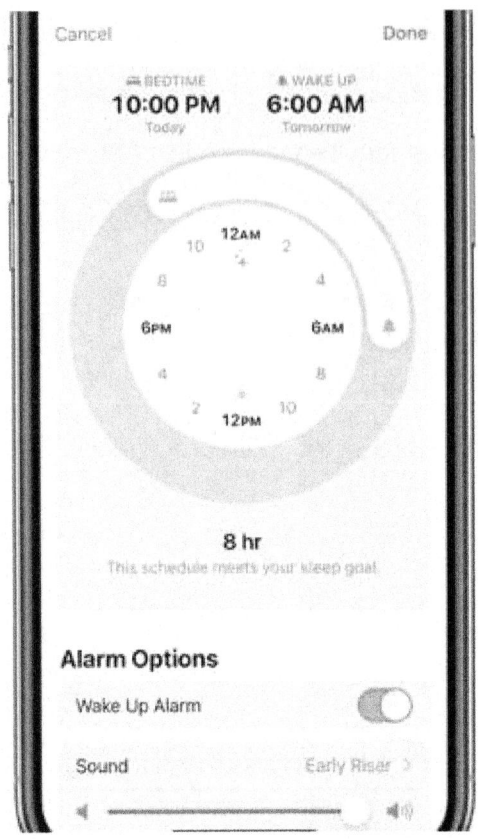

Add or Change a Sleep Schedule

- Click the **Browse** tab, then select **Sleep**.

- Scroll to **Your Schedule,** and tap **Full Schedule & Options.**

- To change a sleep schedule, click **Edit** for the desired schedule.

- To add a new sleep schedule, select **Add Schedule for Other Days.**

- Then tap a day at the top of your screen to remove or add it to your schedule.

- Drag to adjust your Wake Up and for your Bedtime schedule.

- Enable or disable **Wake up Alarm.** If enabled, choose a sound, and set the volume.

- Click **Delete Schedule** at the end of your screen to delete an old schedule, or click **Cancel** at the top of your screen to stop creating a new schedule.

- Tap **Add** or **Done** to save.

Turn Off All Sleep Schedules

- Click the **Browse** tab, then select **Sleep**.

- Scroll to **Your Schedule,** and tap **Full Schedule & Options.**

- Then toggle off **Sleep Schedule** at the top of your screen.

Change Your Wind Down Activities and Schedule

Wind down activities is what you do before bedtime. These include listening to music, reading, etc. The Wind Down shortcuts you choose will appear on your lock screen when your phone is in Sleep Mode.

- Click the **Browse** tab, select **Sleep,** then tap **Full Schedule & Options.**

- To modify when to turn on the Sleep Mode before the set Bedtime, click **Wind Down** and then choose a time.

- To remove or add an activity for winding down, click **Wind Down Shortcuts,** then tap ⊖ to remove or tap **Add Another Shortcut** to include a new activity.

Change Sleep Goal

- Click the **Browse** tab, select **Sleep,** then tap **Full Schedule & Options.**

- To modify the sleep goal, click **Sleep Goal,** and choose a time.

- To turn on other options, tap **Options** and modify as you please.

View Your Sleep History

Sleep history will give you insights into your sleep habits.

- Click the **Browse** tab, and select **Sleep.**
- Click a tab at the top of your screen to see sleep data for a week or month.
- Swipe the graph right or left to change the displayed period.
- Click the column for a day to view details for that day.
- Tap **Add Data** at the top of your screen to manually input sleep data.
- Tap **Show More Sleep Data** to view cumulative sleep data.

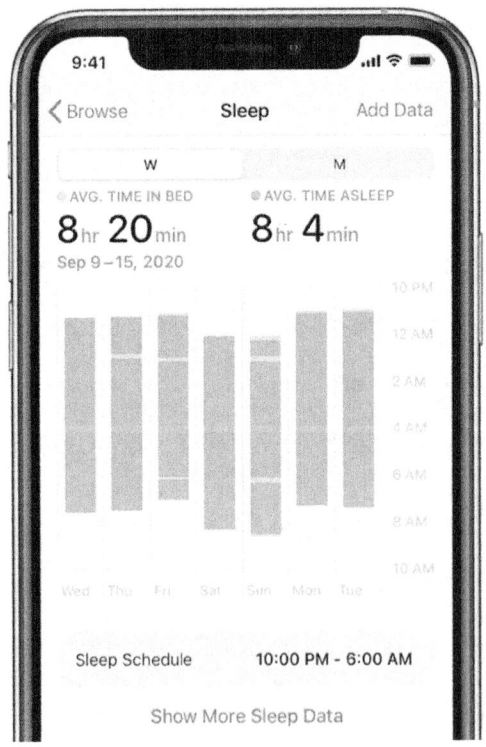

Chapter 32: Translate Text and Voice

Use the Translate app to translate text and voice on your phone. The app allows you to translate conversations and download specific languages to use for translations offline.

Translate Your Voice or Text

- Open the Translate app, rotate the phone to portrait orientation, then click the Translate tab at the bottom of your screen.

- At the top of your screen, select the default language (first button) and tap **Done.** Select the language you want to translate to (second button) and tap **Done.**

- Input your search term in the **Enter Text** field, then tap **Go** on your keyboard. Or click ![mic] , then say a phrase.

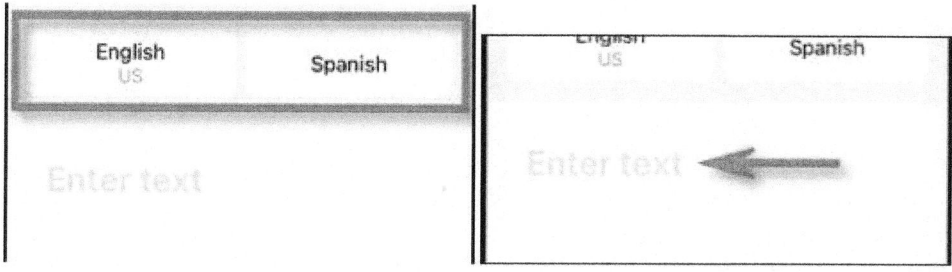

- The translation will show on your screen. Tap ![play] to play the translation audio, and ![star] to save the translation to the Favorite tab.

- Click ![book] to switch to Dictionary mode, then tap each word in a translation to see its meaning.

- Click the Favorite tab to see your saved phrases and history.

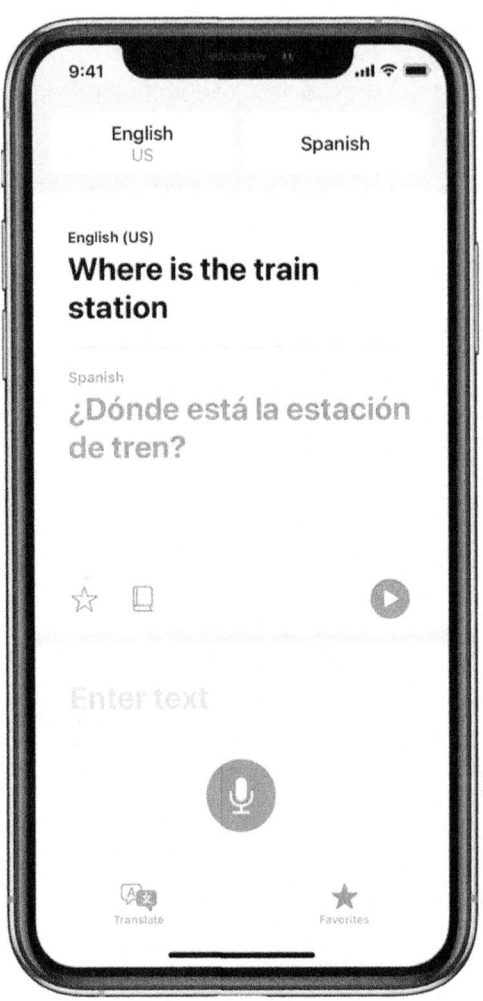

Translate a Conversation

Another amazing feature of the Translate app is the Conversation mode. This mode allows you and another person to hold a conversation in your different languages while the iPhone acts as a translator. You can also download languages to use with the conversation mode when your phone is offline.

The first step is to let your phone know that it should detect the different languages spoken in the conversation. To set this,

- Click on the Default language button on the app's home screen.
- Then scroll to the end of the page and turn on **Automatic Detection.**

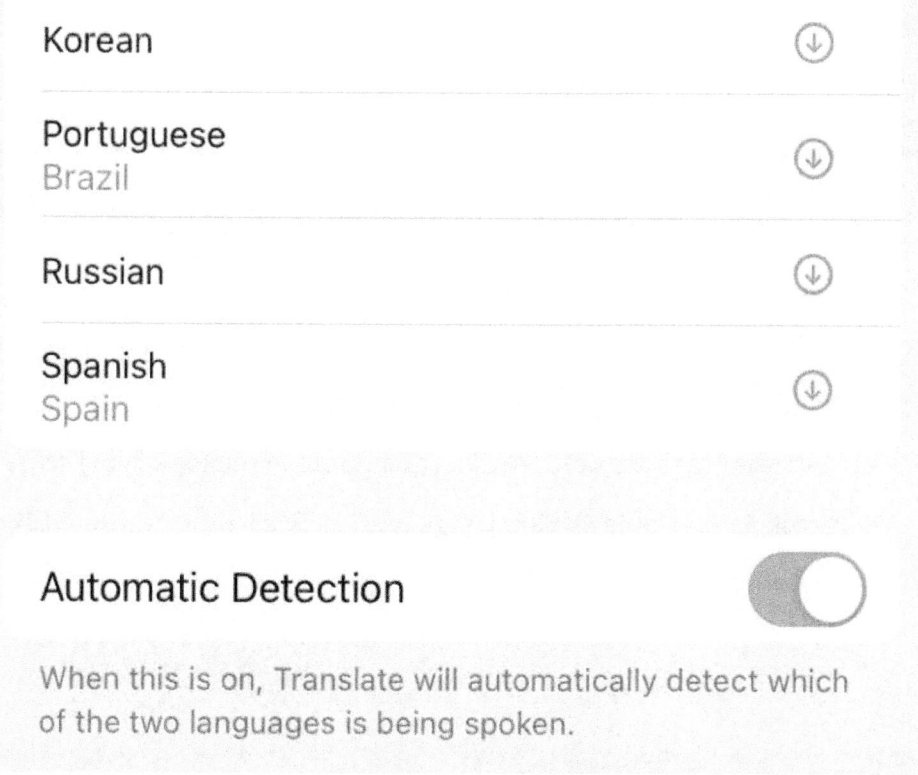

Korean

Portuguese
Brazil

Russian

Spanish
Spain

Automatic Detection

When this is on, Translate will automatically detect which of the two languages is being spoken.

- Once done, rotate your phone to landscape mode, and tap the icon when each person wants to speak.
- The iPhone will automatically translate all the spoken languages. You can also see the whole thread of your conversations on your screen. Scroll up to see the conversation history at any time during the conversation.

Download Languages for Offline Translation

You can download languages to your phone to use when you do not have an active internet connection.

- Click the Translate tab and select a language at the top of your screen.

- Scroll to **Available Offline Languages,** click a language you wish to download, then click **Done.**

Chapter 33: App Store

Use the App Store on iPhone to read featured stories, discover new apps, and learn tips and tricks.

Download an App

- Open the App Store, click an app to view more details, then tap GET to download free apps or tap the price for Paid apps.

  If the ⬇ icon appears rather than the price, it means you already purchased the app. You may download it without paying another fee.

- Authenticate with your passcode or Face ID to complete the purchase.

Share or Give an App

- Click on an app to view its details, then tap ⬆ and choose **Gift App** or choose a sharing option.

Redeem iTunes and App Store Gift Card

You can either purchase a gift card or redeem a gift card on your iPhone.

- Open the App Store and tap your profile picture at the top right.

- Then choose either **Send Gift Card by Email** or **Redeem Gift Card or Code.**

Use App Clips

An app clip is a small part of an app that allows you to perform tasks quickly without downloading and installing the complete app. You can find app clips in Maps, Messages, Safari, or even in the real word when you want to order food, pay for parking, etc. After you discover an app clip, follow any of the steps below to open it:

- Click the app clip link in Messages, Maps, or Safari.
- Use your phone camera to scan the QR code shown at a physical location.
- Place your phone close to the near-field communications tag.

You will see the app clip card at the bottom of your screen.

To find app clips you used recently,

- Go to the home screen and then swipe left until you get to the end of your Home screen pages to access the App library.
- Then tap **Recently Added** to view your app clips.

Remove App Clips

- Go to Settings, tap **App Clips,** then click **Remove All App Clips.**

Manage Your Subscriptions

- Open the App Store and click your profile picture at the top right, then click **Subscriptions.**

Change App Store Settings

To change the settings,

- Go to Settings, tap **App Store,** turn on **Apps** under **Automatic Downloads** to automatically download purchases apps from your other Apple devices.
- Turn on **App Updates** to automatically update your apps.
- Toggle on **Video Autoplay** to automatically play app preview videos.
- Scroll to **Cellular Data** and turn on **Automatic Downloads** to allow the phone to use your cellular data for downloads. To choose to receive a request for permission to download over 200MB or all apps, click **App Downloads.**
- Toggle on **Offload Unused Apps** to have the iPhone automatically remove unused apps.

Prevent in-App Purchases

First, turn on content and privacy restrictions, then do the following:

- Go to Settings, tap **Screen Time,** tap **Content & Privacy Restrictions,** and then click **Content Restrictions.**
- Set your desired restrictions for Apps, App Clips, and iTunes & App Store Purchases.

Chapter 34: Subscribe to Apple Arcade

Apple Arcade offers you unlimited access to several collections of games. You can also share your subscription with up to five other family members at no additional charge. To subscribe,

- Open the App Store and tap **Arcade.**
- Then tap **Subscribe** to begin a monthly subscription or tap **Try it Free** to begin a free one-month subscription.
- Go through the details and then authorize your purchase with your Apple ID or Face ID.

Cancel Apple Arcade Subscription

- Open App Store and click your profile picture at the top right, then click **Subscriptions.**
- Click **Apple Arcade,** then click **Cancel Subscription.**

Find and Download Games

To find and download games on your phone, Open the App Store, then click any of the tabs below:

- **Arcade** to view all the available games in Apple Arcade.
- **Games:** to see the top charts, explore new releases or browse by category.
- **Search:** enter your search term and then click **Search** on your keyboard.

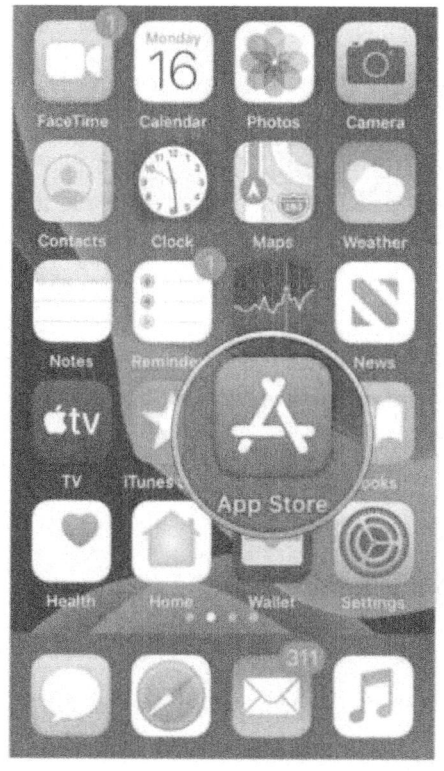 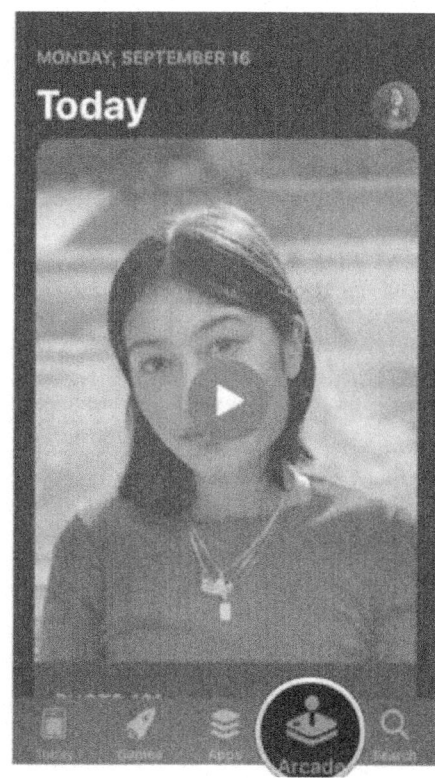

To buy a game,

- Tap **Get** or tap the price. When the game is done downloading, tap **Play** to begin playing.

- When you download games on your phone, you will find the game icon on your home screen. You may click on the game icon to open the game and start playing.

Play with Your Friends on Game Center

Use the Game Center to manage your public profile, send friend requests, and track your scores across your Apple devices.

- Go to Settings, tap **Game Center,** and then sign in with your Apple ID.

- To create a profile, tap **Nickname** and choose a name for yourself.

- Tap **Edit** at the top of your screen to personalize your profile picture. You can use an existing Memoji, create a new Memoji, or edit how your initials appear.
- To invite friends, tap **Friends,** click **Add Friends,** and then input the Apple ID or phone number of your friend or tap ⊕ to choose from your contact list.
- Ask the recipient to click the link in their message to accept the request.

To remove a friend,

- Go through your list of friends and tap **Remove Friend.**

Set Game Center Restrictions

Restrictions include adding friends, multiplayer games, private messaging, and more.

- Go to Settings, tap **Screen Time,** tap **Content & Privacy Restrictions,** and then toggle on **Content & Privacy Restrictions.**
- Click **Content Restrictions,** scroll to **Game Center,** and set your restrictions.

Other Books By Nobert Young

- Apple Watch Series 6 User Guide

  https://www.amazon.com/dp/B08JDTRJXP

- Samsung Galaxy S20 User Guide for Beginners

  https://www.amazon.com/dp/B085DRDXJZ

- Samsung Galaxy Note 20 User Guide

  https://www.amazon.com/dp/B08G54JN8G

- DeepFake Technology: Complete Guide to Deepfakes, Politics

  and Social Media https://amzn.to/2LddlFk

- Senior's Guide to the Samsung Galaxy S20

  https://www.amazon.com/dp/B085R6JM1G

- Senior's Guide to the Samsung Galaxy Note 20

  https://www.amazon.com/dp/B08G571T5H

- Apple TV App User Guide

  https://www.amazon.com/dp/B07ZN8J1B3

- Beginner's Guide To The Apple Airpods Pro

  https://www.amazon.com/dp/1704860962

- Beginner's Guide to the Samsung Galaxy Tab S7 & S7 Plus

  https://www.amazon.com/dp/B08HVDD1BL

- Senior's Guide To The Apple Airpods Pro

  https://www.amazon.com/dp/B07ZXY29DF

Printed in Great Britain
by Amazon

63353019R10141